W9-BXQ-761

THE ASIAN PLAYS

THE ASIAN PLAYS

Fanshen, Saigon, A Map of the World

DAVID HARE

faber and faber
LONDON · BOSTON

This collection first published in 1986 by
Faber and Faber Limited
3 Queen Square London WC1N 3AU

Printed in the United States of America

CONTENTS

INTRODUCTION

The plays in this collection span eight years' writing, so it is important to make clear I am not a playwright who works to a plan. It is Messrs Faber who have pointed out to me that these three plays belong together, just as three plays about England seemed to fit in a previous volume. Each of these children has a very different mother. In my introduction to *The History Plays* I suggested that a writer has little idea why he is drawn to a particular time and place. Asian characters feature also in *Wetherby* and *Plenty*. When I rang the Burmese Embassy in London for details of the national dress for the character of M. Aung in *Plenty*, I was answered by a hostile Third Secretary who demanded 'Why pick on us?'. It was not a question I was easily able to answer.

Nor am I an expert on Asia. If you write at all about the East, you attract such gratitude from people who live there that your own ignorance can seem shaming. Certainly I have travelled there, but temperamentally I am so opposed to the idea that research will of itself validate a work of the imagination that I move about more to set me thinking, than with any idea that wisdom can be acquired by documentary means. There are, after all, package tours to the East these days. Anyone may go and describe what apparently is there. But a little travel teaches you that the Westerner, however peripherally, must always be present in your view of things. To claim to see the world through Asian eyes is, to me at least, transparently absurd.

Fanshen, in fact, is the only one of these three plays with no white man in it, for it dramatizes a book by an American whose understanding of China is profound. William Hinton went as a tractor technician both to observe and help the great land re-

INTRODUCTION

form programmes of the late 1940s. Like a nineteenth-century novelist he made it his business to know a great deal about everything. He brings his understanding of politics, economics, medicine, military strategy, the law, history, agriculture and literature to bear on his study of the single village of Long Bow. When, in 1974, Bill Gaskill and Max Stafford-Clark asked me to adapt the book for the recently-formed Joint Stock company it was plain to us we had no chance of presenting the book with anything like its original scope. In our preliminary workshop we cast around for a method of making a play, sometimes not quite noticing that a rather good method might be suggested by the book we were working on. But slowly the rehearsal methods took their shape from the political techniques which had been developed in the revolution. It became important to the directors that the production be genuinely democratic. An early intimation of this came when Bill insisted as we returned from lunch to our Pimlico rehearsal room that neither he, Max nor I should be the ones to suggest resuming work that afternoon. We would wait until an actor suggested it. I think we waited about an hour and a half.

After the workshop I went off by myself and spent four months fashioning a text. Perversely perhaps, I threw away much of the more obviously dramatic material. I was not interested in portraying the scenes of violence and brutality which marked the landlords' regime and its overthrow. The work we had done with the actors had little influence on me in shaping the play, but I was crucially affected by its spirit. It was Bill Gaskill's overwhelming priority that we should do these people justice. Although the subject matter was political, the instincts of the company were in essence moral. Everyone sensed an obligation to portray Chinese peasants in a way which was adequate to their suffering. The adoption of a rehearsal process based on the Chinese method of self report, public appraisal might, in other hands and with other material, have degenerated into a gimmick. But here it had weight and was surprisingly quick and effective. For the actors, self-criticism was real.

viii

INTRODUCTION

The play opened in Sheffield to a refreshingly intelligent and multi-racial audience, then came to London. Hinton had hitherto ignored it, assuming it would vanish as quickly as two previous dramatic versions. But when he read the reviews, he appeared from a plane almost at once. He consulted with his daughter who had been a Red Guard and then with officials from the Chinese Embassy before insisting that the play must be altered if its life was to be prolonged. He had a list of 110 changes most of which—I am using shorthand here—sought to rid the play of what he called my 'liberal' slant and to give it more of what I would call his 'Marxist' emphasis. A generous and decent man, he also proved an excellent host at his farmhouse in Pennsylvania, as we set off on two days of attritional argument, which resulted in my once or twice giving the play a slightly more optimistic tilt. A line about justice which I had hitherto held to be a fulcrum was removed. The play still stood. If I ever felt resentful about this, I had only to remind myself that his original notes had twice been seized, once by the US Customs and then again by the Senate. The writing of the book had taken him fifteen years. I had given barely six months.

I tried in *Fanshen* to write a classical play about revolution, setting out the problems which will always arise when people try to change the relationship between leadership and the led. A European audience is asked to examine a process of change which is very different from anything which they might anticipate. But I try to retain every situation with which they might identify. Unfailingly, the audience leans forward in scenes during which wealth is to be re-distributed. Everyone wants to know what the criteria are, for they are all thinking about how they will fare when the moment comes. Once, in a phrase which I now think both pretentious and unfortunate, I called *Fanshen* a play for Europe. (It summons up memories of Katie Boyle and 'Luxembourg: *deux points'.*) But I hope readers will know what I meant.

ix

INTRODUCTION

I never used *Fanshen* as an excuse to go to China, for I felt that a quick visit would simply be frustrating. Also, to be honest, if I have written about something, I tend to lose interest in it. Orson Welles said when he passed locations where he had filmed, the buildings stood like blackened teeth from which he had sucked all the goodness. For this reason, and a dozen others, I have never been back to Saigon, which now wears the thin disguise of Ho Chi Minh City. I had spent a very happy time there at the end of 1973, during the phoney peace which ran from the Paris agreement to the final collapse in 1975. During this period, the government were keen to encourage tourism. The beaches at Vung Tau, which were still in parts mined and ringed with barbed wire were being advertised on unlikely posters as being among South-East Asia's finest. I did once bump into a single party of Japanese men with cameras, who, apart from me, seemed to be the only people taking advantage of the tourist programme. I was travelling around in buses trying to get as far into Vietnam as I could at exactly the time that so many Americans finally succeeded in managing to get out.

It took me a long time to find a way of writing about Vietnam, and when I did I was much influenced by a number of films which represented the war as an exclusively American tragedy. We were repeatedly told that Vietnam was a traumatic experience for Americans, but there seemed less regard—at least in fiction—for the Vietnamese themselves. I was determined that the balance of my story would be different. The senior bank teller Quoc gives the film its flavour, and the plight of the local employees at the end provides it, I hope, with its kick. I also tried to be true to my memory of one of the most beautiful cities in the world. It is hard to explain to people who never went there that even during the war life was extraordinarily pleasant for quite large numbers of people. By the time I got there, it was clear this life would soon come to an end, and yet by some act of mass suspension, nobody ever referred to this fact. This, combined of course with the pleasures of the city, gave life a dreamy quality which was rather delicious, even when, as in the first part of the film, the kerosene dumps were exploding on the horizon. As soon as I realized that the American Ambassador had been, literally, unable to imagine a US defeat, I was able to begin writing. But it was not until I understood the behaviour of certain CIA agents, and appreciated that the CIA was regarded in certain parts of Washington as a dangerously liberal organization, that I knew how I would be able to present those final few months.

The making of *Saigon: Year of the Cat* was famously prolonged and difficult. Long before filming began, I was called in Sydney, Australia, and ordered to Bangkok where, I was told, the director was pretending to be ill. When I got there, the producer told me that Stephen Frears was a notoriously lazy and capricious man, and that the doctor had declared that he was simply 'tired'. It was to be my job to persuade him from his bed. As soon as I walked into his ice-cold room I knew at once that the doctor was a fool. I had Stephen moved to the English hospital, where pneumonia was quickly diagnosed. Far from being lazy, Stephen was insistent on working. He called a production conference in which he kept asking the art director about various sequences which did not appear to be in the script. The production team had only just met their director, and did not like to question him. They nodded enthusiastically when he called, as he did obsessively, for 'burning sampans'. It was only after we left the hospital room that I was able to explain to everyone that the director was delirious.

This was why I took a closer part than is usual for a writer in the preparation of the film. I also had to be present throughout its shooting, for we had employed a leading man who was reluctant to say any of the lines I had written. Mercifully, this is the only time I have experienced this problem. Frederic Forrest had worked with Marlon Brando on *Apocalypse Now,* and in his hotel room he played me a video of the long last scene ('The horror! The horror!'), constantly interjecting 'I wrote this', or, more often, 'Marlon wrote this'. This film had convinced him that actors should write their own dialogue. It was more spontaneous. When I pointed out that this was much the worst scene in the film, he seemed not at all disturbed. My blood was chilled when he produced a school exercise book, on one side of which he had written out my entire text in painful longhand, and on the other, what he was actually proposing to say.

We began filming without having resolved the matter. This made life especially hard for Judi Dench whose method, you might say, is the very opposite to Freddy's. She will accept whatever rubbish you throw at her and turn it to gold. In *Saigon* she gives the loveliest of all her screen performances, silkenly sexy and intelligent as only she can be. Although Freddy's rewritings appeared at first to be arbitrary, it was Stephen who noticed there was a pattern to them. Not only did he want, in a rather Hollywood way, to make his character more likeable (though Hollywood-likeable, to me, is detestable), but he also was trying to steer the text away from showing just how badly the Americans had behaved in the final days. It was, in short, an irony. I was trapped in evidence of the problem I had set out to illustrate. My leading man did not truly believe that the Americans had lost a war.

I liked Frederic immensely. He is a man who is both honest and kind. I also admired his acting. But life was undeniably tricky. One weekend, exhausted, I took off for Chiang Mai without leaving a number and came back to find a scene had gone to twenty-four takes without one being accepted. When I finally left Bangkok, two weeks before the end of shooting, I walked into an apartment in New York where the phone was already ringing with the news that a strike of technicians at Thames Television in Teddington meant that our film would have to be abandoned incomplete. Nine months later we reassembled at Shepperton and did manage to finish. We used Battersea Park for downtown Saigon.

I was often told that our troubles were of my making. I had tried to stretch British television too far, by writing on a scale with which it could not be expected to cope. I think this is wrong. Stephen Frears taught me the great and difficult rule of film-making, which is never to accept anything with which you are not satisfied. By his fortitude and high standards he pulled this unwieldy project on to the screen. When it was shown an NBC executive who admired it lamented to my agent that it would never be seen on an American network. 'Oh,' she replied. 'You mean because of the politics?' 'No,' he said, 'Because a middle-aged woman is seen in bed with a younger man. That is totally unacceptable.' At such moments British television can be seen to have its strong points.

A Map of the World is a play which argues with itself, a play full of worry and confusion. Clumsy and disparate, it unreels in a strange and unpredictable fashion, switching styles, shifting arguments. For those who want a political play about the Third World, the long passages about fiction may seem frustrating. For the theatrically minded, the approach to character and plot development may seem perverse. Unarguably, I was trying to do too many things at once, and although I have now directed three productions of the play, I cannot ever quite achieve the right balance between the different strands. The best passages are still those which I wrote quickest.

I had been asked by Jim Sharman to contribute something to the 1982 Adelaide Festival, and implicit in his invitation was the hope that I might be moved to write about Australia. He even gave me a title—The Dead Heart. But my exploratory trip, although highly enjoyable, did not get me writing. On the way back my plane landed in Bombay, and my son and I decided to go into town for a few days. As soon as I walked into my hotel, I knew I had found a setting. The management of the Taj Mahal have since been kind enough to write and ask if the play might be staged in their lobby, but I have had to explain that its formal demands make this impossible. A similar invitation from Mrs Gandhi to perform the play at the Commonwealth Prime Ministers' Conference had to be regretfully declined.

I was obviously trying, as best I could, to articulate arguments which are of great importance to developing countries but at

INTRODUCTION

whose mention people in the West feel themselves, for some reason, entitled to glaze over. I deliberately chose a subject to which there was such in-built resistance and determined to make it live in the theatre. In this I was helped by all the work I had done with Hayden Griffin at the National Theatre and outside it, struggling with the problems of how to design epic plays. All too often the real pleasure of epic theatre—the easy movement of time and place—is lost in the gaps while the scenery is changed. In this way the flow is disrupted and the irony you intend by setting adjacent scenes in different styles gets spoilt as stage-hands in black clothing blunder about in the semi-dark. *A Map of the World* is a seamless epic. There are almost no blackouts. The changes themselves are written as part of the action. They have a rhythm which contributes to the meaning of the play.

Adelaide was a perfect place to open. The temperature was over 110 degrees, and the sky was bluer and wider than any-where in the world. The air was bone-dry. We attracted exactly the response we had hoped for. In an ideal production of the play, you find yourself agreeing with whoever has last spoken. The first preview was regularly interrupted by satisfying cries of 'Nonsense' and 'Right on'. M'Bengue, in particular, attracted considerable heat. A disputatious play, *A Map of the World* seeks to sharpen up people's minds, to ask them to remember why they believe what they do. To ask, in fact, whether they still do. Or should. This seems to me one of the things the theatre does well, and in return for those indignant or excited shouts, I am willing to endure a little mess.

FANSHEN

Fanshen was first performed in London by the Joint Stock Theatre Group at the ICA Terrace Theatre, on 22 April 1975.

Company: Philip Donaghy
Paul Freeman
Cecily Hobbs
Roderic Leigh
Tony Mathews
Philip McGough
Pauline Melville
David Rintoul
Tony Rohr

Directors William Gaskill and Max Stafford-Clark
Designer Di Seymour

ACT I

*Fanshen is an accurate historical record of what once happened
in one village four hundred miles south-west of Peking.*

*Every revolution creates new words. The Chinese revolution
created a whole new vocabulary. A most important word in this
vocabulary was 'fanshen'. Literally it means 'to turn the body'
or 'to turn over'. To China's hundreds of millions of landless
and land-poor peasants it meant to stand up, to throw off the
landlord yoke, to gain land, stock, implements and houses. But
it meant much more than this. It meant to enter a new world.
That is why the book is called* Fanshen. *It is the story of how the
peasants of Long Bow built a new world.*

*This version of William Hinton's book should be played with
about nine actors taking the thirty or so parts. There are no sets,
and no lighting cues. It should be performed using authentic
props and costumes. At one end of the acting area is a small
raised platform on which certain scenes are played. The rest of
the acting area thrusts forward into the audience.*

SECTION ONE

*When the audience are in, the actors appear one by one with a
piece of information. Then they begin to work on stage at their
land, or washing, or begging, or watching until they form a
whole picture of the village.*

CH'UNG-LAI'S WIFE: The village of Long Bow is situated four
   hundred miles south-west of Peking. One thousand people
   live there. In 1946 nearly all the people lived off the land.

5

Landlords claimed from fifty to seventy per cent of their tenants' crop in rent. The rate of interest on loans went as high as one hundred per cent every twenty days. I am Ch'ung-lai's wife. I have no land.

CHENG-K'UAN: A family might possess a few sections of house, each section six foot by nine, made of adobe and straw. Each person might own a quilt, a quilted jacket, cotton trousers, cotton shoes. A bowl.

I am Cheng-k'uan. I have one acre.

T'IEN-MING: The soil of Long Bow was poor. Without manure nothing would grow. The main manure was human manure, the foundation of the whole economy.

I am T'ien-ming. I have half an acre.

HU HSUEH-CHEN: Chinese peasant women had their marriages arranged by their parents, and were often sold as children into landlords' households. Only when a woman became a mother-in-law in her own home did she command any power in a household. All the older women had their feet bound when they were young and could only move short distances.

I am Hu Hsueh-chen, beggar. No land.

FA-LIANG: In Long Bow landlords and rich peasants owned two acres or more per head. Middle peasants owned one acre, poor peasants half an acre per head. Hired labourers owned no land at all.

I am Fa-liang, a hired labourer.

SHEN CHING-HO: By far the largest buiding in Long Bow was the Catholic church, a Gothic building built in 1916 by Belgian Catholics. It acted as a bank and orphanage. Many of the poor of Long Bow bought their wives from the orphanage because it was cheaper.

I am Shen Ching-ho, a landlord. Twenty-three acres.

MAN-HSI: For thousands of years China was ruled by emperors. When the Japanese invaded most of the country was controlled by the Nationalist Party, the Kuomintang, under Chiang Kai-shek. Throughout the Japanese occupation, the most successful and only lasting resistance was organized by the Communist Eighth Route Army. By 1945 when the Japanese left, parts of China were controlled by the Nationalists and parts by the Communists. Long Bow was at the edge.

Man-hsi. Half an acre.

YU-LAI: *(Holding up a copy)* This is the book *Fanshen* by William Hinton.*

I am Yu-lai, an ex-bandit.

TUI-CHIN: Literally the word 'fanshen' means to turn the body or to turn over. This is a record of one village's life between 1945 and 1949. Many of the characters are still alive.

(The peasants work. The landlord on the platform watches. Then he leaves.

The house lights go down.)

1

T'IEN-MING *boxes the compass with a megaphone from on top of the church tower.*

T'IEN-MING: There will be a meeting. There will be a meeting today. In the square after the noon meal. There will be a meeting.

(The men look up from their work.)

FA-LIANG: A meeting.

TUI-CHIN: Twenty years ago we had a meeting.

CHENG-K'UAN: About the church, about who owned the vegetable garden.

(TUI-CHIN shrugs and smiles.)

TUI-CHIN: Another meeting.

(They move from work and gather in the square. They squat down and wait till they are joined. Meanwhile the following scene is played simultaneously. KUO TE-YU is being guarded by MAN-HSI. He carries his rifle like a hoe with a red tassel on the end. The scene is played on the platform. T'IEN-MING comes in.)

T'IEN-MING: A battle. Eight miles away. Outside Changchih.

* The actor should give publisher and current price.

7

MAN-HSI: Are we winning?

T'IEN-MING: Not yet.

MAN-HSI: Then we can't go ahead.

T'IEN-MING: Tie him up.

MAN-HSI: T'ien-ming.

T'IEN-MING: Tie him up. We have messages telling us the Eighth Route Army have liberated fifty million people. Three hundred thousand square miles.

MAN-HSI: But for how long?

T'IEN-MING: It doesn't matter. Elsewhere the Japanese are handing over only to the Kuomintang.

(KUO TE-YU moans.)

Be quiet. The Kuomintang are leaving in wartime puppet governments, puppet troops. They even have the Japanese fighting for them against us in places.

MAN-HSI: Then we must wait till we know . . .

T'IEN-MING: The Kuomintang are throwing their troops into regaining the Liberated Areas. Civil war.

MAN-HSI: If it's still going on, the people will be frightened to . . .

T'IEN-MING: What else can we do? Get that leg up.

MAN-HSI: Can't we wait? Can't we wait for victory before we begin?

T'IEN-MING: No. Above our heads?

MAN-HSI: Very good.

T'IEN-MING: Make a show.

(They hoist the trussed KUO TE-YU above their heads.)

There is a crack in history one inch wide. We fought for it and we must use it.

(They hoist KUO TE-YU down from the platform. They carry him out and throw him down in front of the crowd.)

Countrymen. Your eight years' suffering, your eight years at the hands of the Japanese are over. Their troops have gone. Now—revenge on traitors.

(Cheers from the crowd.)

8

Kuo Te-yu was head of the village for the last two years of the Japanese occupation. He was a collaborator.

PEASANTS: Kill him. Rape his mother.

T'IEN-MING: Yes. But with your help.

(MAN-HSI *stands back from the bundle.*)

T'IEN-MING: You all suffered under this man. You all know what he did. I therefore am asking you to speak it out. We are asking for your help. No one has ever asked your help before. Look at him. There's nothing to fear. You can touch him. Everyone here has a grievance, everyone here has the right to accuse, we all have the same thoughts in our heads. Those of us who fought in the resistance are now asking for your help. You must be the ones to beat down traitors, you must accuse. Who will be the first to speak?

(Silence. People move slightly away from the bundle.)

Fa-liang, what are you thinking? Cheng-k'uan? Tui-chin, have you . . .

(Silence.)

Release him.

MAN-HSI: He . . .

T'IEN-MING: Untie the ropes.

(MAN-HSI *starts to undo the bundle. The people watch. Then* YU-LAI *gets up slowly.*)

YU-LAI: Why not just take him up into the hills . . .

T'IEN-MING: No . . .

YU-LAI: And do whatever you want, shoot him, it's your . . .

T'IEN-MING: He must be tried, in public, by the peasants of Long Bow, by the people he's oppressed . . .

YU-LAI: You're just afraid to kill him yourself . . .

(They start speaking simultaneously, each riding over the other's sentences. YU-LAI *lecturing at* T'IEN-MING.)

T'IEN-MING: No . . .

YU-LAI: Because the Kuomintang are eight miles away . . .

T'IEN-MING: I'm asking for your help . . .

YU-LAI: And if they come back . . .

T'IEN-MING: No one has ever asked anything of you before . . .

9

YU-LAI: Then Kuo Te-yu will be reappointed . . .

T'IEN-MING: I am asking you to speak out your memories . . .

YU-LAI: And anyone who has spoken at the meeting today . . .

T'IEN-MING: That's all, to say what we all know . . .

YU-LAI: Anyone who has taken part in the struggle . . .

T'IEN-MING: Just to speak it out.

YU-LAI: Will be shot. Tell them that.

(Pause.)

T'IEN-MING: So what are you saying?

YU-LAI: What are you saying?

T'IEN-MING: Would you prefer to live under the Kuomintang? Would you like Kuo Te-yu reappointed? Your harvest seized, your goods impounded, your friends in the resistance shot? You want to see more of your friends hanged by the hair until their scalp comes away from their skull? *(Pause.)* Then what are you saying?

YU-LAI: I'm saying . . .

T'IEN-MING: Yes?

YU-LAI: Those who accuse collaborators may themselves be killed.

T'IEN-MING: Yes. *(Pause.)* So will you speak first?

(Pause. YU-LAI stuck. T'IEN-MING smiles.)

Wang Yu-lai?

YU-LAI: Don't laugh at me.

T'IEN-MING: I'm not laughing.

YU-LAI: If you . . .

T'IEN-MING: Of course, if you're frightened . . .

YU-LAI: Wait. I'm thinking.

(The villagers smile, enjoying YU-LAI's difficulty. Then slowly he sits down.)

Give me time to think.

(KUO TE-YU is now untied. T'IEN-MING stares hard at the crowd.)

T'IEN-MING: The resistance worked eight years. Some of you . . . silently supported us, in secret. Now the war against the Japanese is over, a civil war may begin. If we cannot beat down the traitors . . . *(He moves towards* KUO.) You're frightened of him. There's nothing. Look. *(He puts his finger inside* KUO's *mouth, between his teeth. Holds it there. Looks at the crowd. Takes it out.)* There's nothing there.

YU-LAI: You've paid him not to bite you.

T'IEN-MING: Come here.

YU-LAI: No.

T'IEN-MING: Come here.

*(*YU-LAI *looks round, then walks up.* T'IEN-MING *places him dead opposite* KUO TE-YU.)*

Was this man a collaborator?

*(*YU-LAI *nods.)*

Did you suffer at his hands?

*(*YU-LAI *nods.)*

Did he steal your harvest?

*(*YU-LAI *nods.)*

Did he butcher your friends?

*(*YU-LAI *nods.)*

Accuse him.

(A pause. Then YU-LAI *strikes* KUO TE-YU *across the face. Then he smashes a fist under his jaw.* KUO TE-YU *falls back. Then* YU-LAI *picks him up, hits him again.)*

Accuse him.

*(*YU-LAI *stands him unsteadily on his feet, then takes a pace back.)*

YU-LAI: Shen So-tzu was tortured for eighteen days, starved and shot. He was responsible. He betrayed him to the Japanese. I saw the body. I know it happened.

T'IEN-MING: Name him.

YU-LAI: Kuo Te-yu.

*(*YU-LAI *goes back and takes his place in the crowd. Silence. Then a voice from a man still sitting in the crowd.)*

CHENG-K'UAN: Kung Lai-pao was cut to pieces with a samurai sword.

T'IEN-MING: Stand up.

CHENG-K'UAN: *(Stands)* It was his treachery. Kuo Te-yu.

11

FA-LIANG: I was made to hand over three bags of grain or told the Japanese would burn my whole crop. He took it away and kept it.

T'IEN-MING: Name him.

FA-LIANG: Kuo Te-yu.

TUI-CHIN: He sent me to work in the fields, I was never paid. One day . . .

(Then an outbreak of shouting in the crowd, all on top of each other.)

CHENG-K'UAN: Kill the donkey's tool.

TUI-CHIN: Rape his mother.

MAN-HSI: Kill him.

(They all rush forward on KUO TE-YU and start a huge brawl. T'IEN-MING throws himself in to try and protect KUO TE-YU.)

T'IEN-MING: Leave him. Leave him. He's only a puppet.

KUO TE-YU: *(Screaming now)* I carried orders, I was only carrying out orders.

T'IEN-MING: Leave him.

(He manages to clear a space for KUO TE-YU.)

He took orders. Let him testify.

KUO TE-YU: I was told what to do.

YU-LAI: Who told you?

KUO TE-YU: When Ch'i-Yun . . .

T'IEN-MING: Commander of the puppet garrison, Long Bow fort.

KUO TE-YU: Murderer. Killed many in my sight. Shen Chi-mei . . .

T'IEN-MING: Head of Fifth District Police . . .

KUO TE-YU: Killed many. Ordered many dead. Took prisoners. Cut their hands, their fingers. He ran the camps.

(Silence.)

TUI-CHIN: Shoot them.

T'IEN-MING: Nobody will be shot, nobody, until they have been tried by you. You have taken their lives into your hands, you, the peasants of Long Bow. It lies with you. Do you understand?

2

The peasants gather to watch. Still figures. Two men are lined up with sacks over their heads.

T'IEN-MING: Down with traitors, down with Kuomintang agents, liquidate the bloody eight years' debt.

(MAN-HSI cocks his rifle.)

Arrested, tried, found guilty by the people. Wen Ch'i-Yun, commander of the puppet garrison, Long Bow fort. Shen Chi-mei, head of the Fifth District Police.

(MAN-HSI shoots them. They fall. The people watch as T'IEN-MING and MAN-HSI strip the bodies of their clothes. They then hold the clothes out to the people.)

Here. The fruits of struggle. What we have seized from traitors. Take them. You have earned them. You deserve them. You have played your part. You have condemned the traitors, you have executed collaborators.

(The people look at the clothes, but they turn away and will not take them. Then SHEN CHING-HO, the landlord, passes across the back of the stage. They scatter. T'IEN-MING and MAN-HSI are left holding out the goods.)

Take them. Take them.

(There is no one left.)

SECTION TWO

1

Slogan: **Asking Basic Questions**

SECRETARY LIU *appears, to address three cadres from Long Bow:* T'IEN-MING, MAN-HSI *and* YU-LAI. *They sit in a square.*

Slogan: **The Visit of Secretary Liu**

LIU: An island in the centre of China. A province held by the Eighth Route Army. Now—a short ceasefire in the war between the Kuomintang and ourselves. During this time the possibility of a coalition is to be explored. But for a time our

13

ground is safe. Our army protects us. In Lucheng County there is a People's Government. Our duty, the duty of all village leaders, is to consolidate the successes of the Anti-Traitor movement. The history of China is a history of bloody and violent rebellion. But always the blood runs down the gutter and nothing is changed. How are we to make sure this time, in this tight circle, the overturning holds?

The difference is, this time, we think. We ask questions. We analyse. This is why I have come to talk to you. Today you must consider a single question. Who depends upon whom for a living?

MAN-HSI: What's the answer?

LIU: No, you must think.

(T'IEN-MING *gets up and crosses to another part of the stage where he is joined by the peasants from the previous scene:* TUI-CHIN, CH'UNG-LAI'S WIFE, HU HSUEH-CHEN, FA-LIANG. *There are now two meetings which are played antiphonally for the rest of the section.*)

Slogan: **The Forming of the Peasants' Association**

T'IEN-MING: If we peasants are to organize ourselves we must know why. We must start with questions. We must find an answer to the most important question. Who depends upon whom for a living? Well can anyone . . .

MAN-HSI: We depend on the land.

LIU: On whom?

MAN-HSI: On the person who owns the land.

LIU: The landlord.

MAN-HSI: Yes. We depend on the landlord for a living.

LIU: Yu-lai?

MAN-HSI: If the landlord didn't rent us land, we'd starve.

LIU: But who gave him the land?

MAN-HSI: He bought it.

LIU: How did he make the money to buy it?

YU-LAI: If . . .

MAN-HSI: No, let me, leave this to me. It's not . . . Listen . . . I've forgotten what I was going to say.

14

FA-LIANG: Why do we need to know?

T'IEN-MING: You must not just do things. You must know why you do things.

FA-LIANG: Why?

T'IEN-MING: Because you need a theory . . .

TUI-CHIN: What's a theory?

MAN-HSI: The question is . . . I don't see it. Why ask it? What answer do you want? What do you want me to say?

LIU: You must work it out for yourself. If you want to serve the people you need to think.

MAN-HSI: Collaborators, yes, I could understand, should be executed; this, I don't understand.

T'IEN-MING: Fa-liang. Tell us something of your life.

FA-LIANG: My life?

T'IEN-MING: Yes. Just tell us.

FA-LIANG: I was fourteen when I went to work for Shen Ching-ho. My mother had been ill, my father had to borrow four dollars from the landlord to buy medicine. So to guarantee the loan he lent me to the landlord to work for seven years. I was always hungry. Twice I was ill. But no matter how hard I worked I couldn't begin to pay off the debt. By the time I'd worked for him three years, we owed him fifteen dollars instead of four. And then, after seven years, by the time he'd taken off all the things he claimed I'd broken, all the time I was sick, what was left was not enough to pay even the interest on the debt. So I had no wages at all. I had worked seven years. And he gave me nothing. At the end I tore down two sections of our house, I tore out the timbers. And only then could I pay back the original debt.

CH'UNG-LAI'S WIFE: I was told at the age of nine to be Ch'ung-lai's wife. I then had to serve in his family for six years before I married him. I was a child wife, everyone beat me. One day my mother-in-law broke my arm. The water in the pot was boiling. I asked her what I should cook in it. She didn't answer. I asked her again. She picked up an iron poker and broke my arm with it. She said I annoyed her. I lay on the

15

k'ang for a fortnight, couldn't work or move. Then Ch'ung-lai's family threw me out. Ch'ung-lai went to Taiyuan to get work pulling a rickshaw, I went to work as a cook for a land-lord. After about six years we earned enough to buy one acre of land, but it only yielded two bags of grain. After we had paid taxes, there was nothing left.

LIU: Why should one man have the right to say 'This land is mine' and then without doing any work himself demand half of what's grown on it?

MAN-HSI: He owns it. It's his, he can do what he likes.

LIU: Is it right?

MAN-HSI: Listen. I work for a landlord. He feeds me. At the end of the year he pays me. If he had cheated me, then I could . . . discuss it with you. But as he doesn't . . . then . . . so.

LIU: So tell me. Who depends on whom?

MAN-HSI: It's . . .

YU-LAI: I . . .

MAN-HSI: Say the thing again.

LIU: Who depends on whom?

T'IEN-MING: Hsueh-chen.

HSUEH-CHEN: My father was a labourer but he sold me to a husband against my will. My husband could find no work, could barely live. So he gambled what money we had. We lost our only quilt, we were left with nothing. I've had three children. One I saw the Japanese kill, a soldier with his boot, then with his sword. The second died of worms crawling out of him. So I threw my husband out of the house, took my third child, begged alone. People give me nothing. I live in the fields, eat herbs, sleep in the straw. And my third child is alive.

MAN-HSI: There has to be somebody to give us work to do.

YU-LAI: Why?

MAN-HSI: If there were no landlords we'd starve.

TUI-CHIN: I once went to my landlord to ask for more wages. He said, if you're poor it's because the heavens will it, it's because your grave is poorly located. All you can do is wait for

16

your luck to change. Select a more suitable spot for your own grave and hope that the eight ideographs of earth and heaven are in better conjunction when your son is born.

T'IEN-MING: What do you conclude?

Slogan: **They Talked For Eight Hours**

T'IEN-MING: We have all suffered. But we've never asked why. If we had to suffer. Do you see?

MAN-HSI: I don't understand.

Slogan: **They Talked For Three Days**

T'IEN-MING: Think. All think of your lives. Think what you've endured, what have you suffered for?

YU-LAI: What can they do which we can't? Nothing. What can we do which they can't? We can work. Our labour transforms their land. We make it valuable, we create their wealth.

CH'UNG-LAI'S WIFE: We have all suffered for them.

T'IEN-MING: So who depends on whom?

YU-LAI: We make them rich, they depend on our labour, they depend on us.

CH'UNG-LAI'S WIFE: They depend on us.

T'IEN-MING: Yes.

LIU: Yes.

FA-LIANG: They depend on us.

YU-LAI: Take us away, they'd die. Take them away, we live.

T'IEN-MING: You do not depend on them. They depend on you. Understand this and everything you have ever known is changed.

LIU: We have liberated a peach tree heavy with fruit. Who is to be allowed to pick the fruit? Those who have tended and watered the tree? Or those who have sat at the side of the orchard with folded arms?

YU-LAI: We shouldn't even pay rent.

Slogan: **They Stopped Paying Rent**

LIU: The policy in the Liberated Areas is to ask simply for a reduction in rents and interest charges. But here in Lucheng County, you—the leaders—will go ahead of the policy.

17

FANSHEN

(They shake hands with LIU *and say good-bye. Then join the peasants.)*

T'IEN-MING: Now surely we can right the wrongs of the past. Already in many places the landlords have been beaten down. We have only to follow the example of others. Then we can all fanshen.

(Above the platform they raise a red banner saying FAN-SHEN.)

SECTION THREE

1

Slogan: **Settling Accounts**

At one end CH'UNG-WANG *sits with a pair of scales, ready to receive rent. At the other on the platform* CHING-HO *sits, with his fingernails being tended by his* DAUGHTER.

CHING-HO: Shen Ching-ho. A landlord.

CH'UNG-WANG: Kuo Ch'ung-wang. A landlord.

(A group of peasants form outside CH'UNG-WANG*'s house. Then* TUI-CHIN *steps from the group and into the house.)*

CH'UNG-WANG: Rent.

TUI-CHIN: The peasants have decided to stop paying rent.

CH'UNG-WANG: Come here.

TUI-CHIN: We have decided it's wrong to pay rent. And we have decided you took too much in the past . . .

CH'UNG-WANG: Come here.

TUI-CHIN: Through the war, you charged us too much. And we want it back.

CH'UNG-WANG: Tui-chin, the land you farm . . .

TUI-CHIN: Also interest on loans, that was too high . . .

CH'UNG-WANG: You have just lost.

TUI-CHIN: And we want that back. And land you seized when we couldn't pay our debts . . .

CH'UNG-WANG: The house you live in . . .

18

TUI-CHIN: We want that back. Also there are to be penalties for when you hit us . . .
CH'UNG-WANG: You have just lost.
TUI-CHIN: Or abused us or starved us . . .
CH'UNG-WANG: The clothes you are wearing . . .
TUI-CHIN: If it's wrong to pay rent . . .
CH'UNG-WANG: You have just lost.
TUI-CHIN: It must always have been wrong.
CH'UNG-WANG: Come here.

(CH'UNG-WANG *rises to strike* TUI-CHIN. *At once the villagers invade the house.*)

CHENG-K'UAN: Elected Chairman, Peasants' Association.
YU-LAI: Elected Vice-Chairman, Peasants' Association. Find his grain.
CH'UNG-WANG: Peasants' Association?

(FA-LIANG *goes out to search for his grain.*)

YU-LAI: You are to attend a meeting at which your past life will be reviewed. Everything you have taken from us unfairly since the war began—rent, interest, land—you will return. Everything you have done to us since the Japanese came you will pay for. In one day we will add up the bill for your life.
FA-LIANG: Look.
YU-LAI: Until then we are seizing your grain as security for your debt. And we are posting militia on your land.

(FA-LIANG *returns, throwing down a rotten bag of mildewed grain.*)

FA-LIANG: Look. Look.
TUI-CHIN: It's rotten. Why? Why did you let it go rotten? How could you?
FA-LIANG: This was salt.
TUI-CHIN: Salt. This was salt. *(He takes the jar and flings the contents in* CH'UNG-WANG's *face. It has hydrolized.)* One year when I couldn't pay my rent you took my whole harvest. Now I find it's in here rotting. Why?
YU-LAI: He was hoarding it. He was hoping to make money.
FA-LIANG: People died . . .

19

YU-LAI: Wait . . .

TUI-CHIN: Le-miao starved to death on your land . . .

YU-LAI: Wait . . .

TUI-CHIN: All the time this was here.

FA-LIANG: Once I came begging, I crawled for grain . . .

YU-LAI: Wait . . .

TUI-CHIN: Kill him. Cut off his hands.

YU-LAI: Wait. Wait for the meeting.

Slogan: **Fifty-eight Accusations**

(The group re-forms. The other villagers go, leaving just FA-LIANG, TUI-CHIN, CHENG-K'UAN *and* YU-LAI *facing* CH'UNG-WANG.)

YU-LAI: The people have accused you. Now you must pay.

FA-LIANG: There are six good bags of grain. That's all I can find.

CHENG-K'UAN: It's not enough.

TUI-CHIN: We've measured his land. Thirteen acres.

CHENG-K'UAN: Not enough.

YU-LAI: He owes the village one hundred bags of grain. It's his blood debt. And his sweat debt. He must settle accounts.

CHENG-K'UAN: Look. Here is a list of everything you took from us. Where is it?

CH'UNG-WANG: I don't know.

FA-LIANG: You turned it into coins.

CH'UNG-WANG: I don't have any coins.

FA-LIANG: All your houses, all your stock, all your grain, your clothes are not enough to settle your account. Where are your coins?

CH'UNG-WANG: No coins.

FA-LIANG: Where are they?

*(*YU-LAI *clears a space. He hits* CH'UNG-WANG *twice.)*

CH'UNG-WANG: Fifty dollars. In the stove.

YU-LAI: Fa-liang. Stove.

*(*FA-LIANG *goes off.* YU-LAI *nods at* CHENG-K'UAN.)*

YU-LAI: Cheng-k'uan.

*(*CHENG-K'UAN *moves round for his turn. Hits* CH'UNG-WANG.)*

20

CH'UNG-WANG: Forty dollars.

CHENG-K'UAN: Where?

CH'UNG-WANG: Back yard.

YU-LAI: Fa-liang. Back yard.

(YU-LAI *nods now at* TUI-CHIN *who takes his turn at hitting* CH'UNG-WANG.)

CH'UNG-WANG: Thirty. Under the stable.

YU-LAI: Fa-liang. Stable. *(He turns and smiles at* TUI-CHIN.) All right?

TUI-CHIN: Yes.

YU-LAI: May we leave it to you?

TUI-CHIN: Of course.

YU-LAI: It may be slow.

CHENG-K'UAN: Good night.

YU-LAI: Good night.

(They smile and go off. TUI-CHIN *looks at* CH'UNG-WANG, *then kicks him again.* SHEN CHING-HO *rises.)*

CH'UNG-WANG: Another fifteen. Under the tree.

TUI-CHIN: Fa-liang. Tree.

(On the platform CHING-HO *suddenly speaks.)*

CHING-HO: My oldest clothes. *(He changes and dirties his hands.)* One bag of white flour.

(His DAUGHTER *fetches it. He turns to her.)*

Kiss me.

(She does so. Then they set off across the village. FA-LIANG *returns with the coins.)*

TUI-CHIN: Did you get them?

FA-LIANG: Yes.

(They look at each other.)

TUI-CHIN: When I was born my family wanted to celebrate. But they had to borrow money for dumplings. And so before I could speak, I was already in debt to the landlord. A man stands up to his neck in water, so that even a ripple is enough to drown him.

(The scene scatters, as CHING-HO *stops at the door of* YU-LAI *and* CHENG-K'UAN *who are sitting at home. He puts the bag*

21

down and gestures to his DAUGHTER *to stay outside, unseen.
Then he goes in.)*

CHING-HO: New Year.

YU-LAI: Yes.

CHING-HO: I had to come.

(He smiles. YU-LAI *looks at* CHENG-K'UAN.)

A new life. Just to say a Happy New Year, a happy new life.

YU-LAI: Yes.

CHING-HO: That's good. Thank you. *(He goes to the door, slips
his hand out, brings in the bag.)* I know your life is hard. On
this soil. The valuable work you are doing. Service to the
community. But we are all . . . citizens of one village. Please
no ceremony but . . . help yourselves to the flour and pass a
Happy New Year. *(He puts the bag down and walks backwards away.)* If at any time you should meet any difficulty in
your new life in any way you should know my door is as it has
always been, open, and I am as I have always been, ready to
help. *(He gestures his* DAUGHTER *in.)* This is my daughter.
She has always wanted to . . .

(Silence.)

Yours. Good night. *(He goes out.)*

(YU-LAI *and* CHENG-K'UAN *look at each other. The* DAUGHTER
stands silent, dignified, ignored for the rest of the scene.)

YU-LAI: What does he take us for? Rats who can be bought for
one bag of flour? One bag? I'm worth a thousand bags. I am a
granary.

(CHENG-K'UAN *looks at the impassive girl, then goes over to
the flour, puts a finger in, licks it, then stares in the bag as
down a deep well.)*

The richest landlord in Long Bow. In the famine year he gave
us nothing, now suddenly we all belong to one village. And
we are offered flour.

(T'IEN-MING *appears on the platform.)*

T'IEN-MING: Never trust a landlord, never protect a landlord.
There is only one road and that is to struggle against them.

(A banner descends reading: **Never Trust A Landlord, Never**

Protect A Landlord, There Is Only One Road And That Is To
Struggle Against Them)

2

CHING-HO *is seized as he goes home, stripped, tortured. Silent
tableaux of the scene as it is described.*

MAN-HSI: When the final struggle began Ching-ho was faced
with accusations from more than half the village. Old women
who had never spoken in public before stood up to accuse
him. Altogether one hundred and eighty people testified.
Ching-ho had no answer to any of them. When the Association met to decide what he owed, it came to four hundred
bags of grain.

CHENG-K'UAN: That evening all the people went to Ching-ho's
courtyard to help take over his property. It was very cold. We
built bonfires and the flames shot up towards the stars. It was
very beautiful.

YU-LAI: We dug up all his money, beating him, digging, finding
more, beating him, digging, finding more. By the time the
sun was rising in the sky we had five hundred dollars.

T'IEN-MING: We were all tired and hungry. We decided to eat
all the things Ching-ho had prepared for the New Year. There
was a whole crock full of dumplings stuffed with pork and
peppers. We even had shrimp. Everyone ate their fill and
didn't notice the cold.

SHEN CHING-HO: Of the seven landlords in Long Bow, three
died after being beaten to death by the Peasants' Association.
Two more died of starvation when they had been driven from
their land. Shen Ching-ho was luckier: he ran away and became a teacher in a primary school.

3

Slogan: **Distribution of Fruits**
YU-LAI *speaks from on high.* T'IEN-MING *stands beside him.*
CHENG-K'UAN *organizes the peasants while* MAN-HSI *counts
with an abacus.*

YU-LAI: We have seized the wealth from fifteen families. Two hundred and eighty-six acres of land, twenty-six draft animals, four hundred sections of house. And behind the temple doors: everything they own.

(The peasants stand in single file while CHENG-K'UAN *explains.)*

CHENG-K'UAN: You'll be given a number.

FA-LIANG: Yes.

CHENG-K'UAN: The number will be the number of pounds of grain you've been allocated.

FA-LIANG: Yes.

CHENG-K'UAN: You may then either keep the grain or change it into any object you want from inside the temple. Each object has its price marked on it. A plough I think three hundred-weight of grain. A shovel fifty pounds, a slipper two, a rattle one, so on.

MAN-HSI: A hundred and eighty.

CHENG-K'UAN: You may spend a hundred and eighty pounds of grain.

YU-LAI: *(From above)* The poorest allowed in first.

CHENG-K'UAN: Ch'ou-har. Because you are poor and have many needs, we have put your number up.

MAN-HSI: A hundred and ninety.

CHENG-K'UAN: You may spend a hundred and ninety pounds of grain.

CH'OU-HAR: A hundred and ninety.

CHENG-K'UAN: Hsueh-chen. Your number is not as high as others. There are only two in your family. We know you suffered a great deal but you did not speak at meetings. You did not speak out your grievances at landlords.

(She nods, too shy to reply.)

CHENG-K'UAN: How can we know unless you speak out? Anyway you've got what you need.

MAN-HSI: One hundred and twenty.

CHENG-K'UAN: You may spend one hundred and twenty pounds of grain. Go in. Next.

TUI-CHIN: Tui-chin.

CHENG-K'UAN: Yes. Now, you have denounced many landlords. You have been active in the struggle from the start, spoken at meetings. This should ensure you a lot. But in every case we have also balanced people's grievances against their needs. And you are a single man, who has a lot of the implements he needs. So your number has come down.

TUI-CHIN: What if I want a cow, but haven't been given enough grain?

CHENG-K'UAN: Then you'll get a share in a cow.

TUI-CHIN: A share?

T'IEN-MING: Yes. Why not?

TUI-CHIN: Share a cow?

T'IEN-MING: Four families, one leg each.

TUI-CHIN: Very good.

MAN-HSI: A hundred and fifty pounds of grain.

CHENG-K'UAN: Next.

CH'UNG-LAI'S WIFE: I am Ch'ung-lai's wife.

CHENG-K'UAN: Yes, yes I know. Many—grievances—yes—and also great need. Grievances and need both high. Man-hsi? *(Pause.)*

CH'UNG-LAI'S WIFE: What do you get?

CHENG-K'UAN: What?

CH'UNG-LAI'S WIFE: The leaders, what do the leaders get? You, the Chairman of the Association. Yu-lai over there, T'ien-ming, village head. What do you get?

T'IEN-MING: The leaders get less.

CH'UNG-LAI'S WIFE: They get some?

T'IEN-MING: They get some but they get less.

(YU-LAI *has been listening to this last exchange.*)

MAN-HSI: Two hundred and ten.

CHENG-K'UAN: Go into the temple. Make your choice.

CH'UNG-LAI'S WIFE: Thank you. Thank you. *(She goes in.)*

(YU-LAI, CHENG-K'UAN *and* T'IEN-MING *are left outside.*)

YU-LAI: Why?

CHENG-K'UAN: Mm?

25

YU-LAI: Why less?

CHENG-K'UAN: Less because . . .

T'IEN-MING: Less because you're the leaders and you must wait for the peasants to suggest you get some.

YU-LAI: Wait for them?

T'IEN-MING: Yes.

YU-LAI: Well it's not worth it. I'd be better off as a peasant.

T'IEN-MING: Yes.

(Pause.)

YU-LAI: I think we should get something. Not for ourselves, more for expenses, for the Association. If we took over the inn, managed it, that would help pay for the school, pay for the oil we need for lamps for Association meetings. We're going to have to make some money somehow.

CHENG-K'UAN: Take over the inn?

YU-LAI: Why not?

(Pause.)

CHENG-K'UAN: Put it to the people.

YU-LAI: I thought we were waiting for them to put it to us.

(They smile.)

CHENG-K'UAN: Take over the inn.

(The peasants begin to come out carrying loot. Some have bags of grain, some implements. FA-LIANG is wearing a landlord's coat.)

HSUEH-CHEN: A quilt! A landlord's quilt!

(TUI-CHIN *comes out with a pot bigger than himself.*)

T'IEN-MING: Are you sure that's what you want?

TUI-CHIN: Certain. I've always wanted it.

FA-LIANG: All my life I have been oppressed and exploited.

TUI-CHIN: For all the grain I'm going to have.

(He embraces T'IEN-MING *crying.* CH'OU-HAR *has a huge bag of grain.)*

CH'OU-HAR: The bad life. The unbearable life of working for others.

CH'UNG-LAI'S WIFE: We are moving from hell to heaven. To live in your own house, to eat out of your own bowl, is the happiest life.

(YU-LAI *looks at* T'IEN-MING *and smiles.*)

SECTION FOUR

1

Night. T'IEN-MING *and* MAN-HSI *walk up and down in silence, guarding the road to Changchih.* T'IEN-MING *choosing his moment.*

Slogan: **The Party**

T'IEN-MING: Comrade. What do you think of the Eighth Route Army?

MAN-HSI: What do I think of it?

(Silence.)

What can I think? I used to have nothing, now I've fanshened. Everything I have the Eighth Route Army gave me.

T'IEN-MING: And the Communist Party?

MAN-HSI: Isn't that the same thing?

T'IEN-MING: Not exactly. The Party organized the army, in the army there are Party members. The Party directs the army, but most of the soldiers aren't in the Party. And it's the Party which led the battle against the landlords.

MAN-HSI: I see. *(He doesn't.)* Where is the Party then, where can you find it?

T'IEN-MING: I . . .

MAN-HSI: Do you know?

T'IEN-MING: Yes.

MAN-HSI: Well?

T'IEN-MING: It's many miles away, some hundreds of miles. In the countryside. Would you come with me?

MAN-HSI: Of course. Let's go. Let's go tomorrow.

T'IEN-MING: It's a long way. And through Kuomintang country. It's difficult. Dangerous.

27

MAN-HSI: It doesn't matter, you say the Party led us to fanshen, so we must find it, let's go.

T'IEN-MING: Don't rush into it. You . . .

MAN-HSI: Go on.

T'IEN-MING: You may be risking your life.

MAN-HSI: Well?

T'IEN-MING: You may be risking your family's life.

MAN-HSI: I've made up my mind.

T'IEN-MING: Man-hsi . . .

MAN-HSI: Why do you talk about danger as if we weren't in danger already?

T'IEN-MING: In that case . . . your journey is over. The Party is here. I am a member of the Communist Party.
(Silence.)

MAN-HSI: Why did you trick me?

T'IEN-MING: Because the Communist Party is an illegal organization.

MAN-HSI: So?

T'IEN-MING: If the enemy returns we will all be killed. Membership is secret. Even if you are arrested and beaten to death, you must never admit you belong.

MAN-HSI: You deceived me.

T'IEN-MING: Listen . . .

MAN-HSI: Who else in Long Bow?

T'IEN-MING: You'd be the first.
(Pause.)

MAN-HSI: What do you hope to do? To take over the village?

T'IEN-MING: Never.

MAN-HSI: What then?

T'IEN-MING: The Party must be the backbone of the village. It must educate, study, persuade, build up the People's organizations—the Peasants' Association, the Village Government, the Women's Association, the People's Militia, it must coordinate all these, give them a clear line to follow, a policy that will unite everyone who can be united. Without the Party the village is a bowl of loose sand. So its members must

get up earlier, work harder, attend more meetings, stay up later than anyone else, worry before anyone else is worried. We must become the best organized, the most serious group in the village. All in secret. We must lead, not by force but by example. By being good people. By being good Communists.
(Pause.)
MAN-HSI: I'd hoped for something . . .
T'IEN-MING: Yes.
(Pause.)
Do you see? Do you see how hard it is? And how far? And how dangerous?

2

In a series of tableaux on the platform HU HSUEH-CHEN, *her husband and* T'IEN-MING *act out the story that* CH'UNG-LAI'S WIFE *tells.*

CH'UNG-LAI'S WIFE: Liberation and the settling accounts movement were to Hu Hsueh-chen what water is to a parched desert. She won clothes and threw away her rags, she won a quilt and threw away her flea-infested straw, she won land and gave up begging. Knowing that these gains were the result of struggle and not gifts from heaven, she attended every meeting and supported those who were active although she herself was afraid to speak in public. Then she met a revolutionary cadre who helped to make her fanshen complete. This man, a doctor, asked for her hand in marriage. She hesitated. She asked for a conference to tell him the whole story of her life. She told him she could not stand any more suffering or oppression at the hands of a man. He persuaded Hu Hsueh-chen that he was a man of principle, and that, most important, as a product of the revolutionary army and its Communist education, he believed in equality for women. They were married in February 1946. Her husband began even to cook his own supper so his wife could attend meetings —something unheard of in Long Bow. She became more active when he explained that fanshen could only be

achieved through struggle. She finally mastered her shyness
and became secretary of the Women's Association.

In late 1946 her husband had to move away. He wrote her
letters urging her to work hard. 'When you run into trouble,
don't be gloomy. For there can be no trouble to compare with
the past.' One day Man-hsi came to talk to her about the
Communist Party. Then later T'ien-ming came and asked her
if anyone had spoken to her on the subject. She knew the
Party was meant to be secret so she denied having been
approached.

A few days later T'ien-ming came back with an application
form and helped her fill it out. He asked if she would give her
life for the Party.

HSUEH-CHEN: I would.

CH'UNG-LAI'S WIFE: And he enrolled her in the Party to which
her husband, unknown to her, had long belonged.

SECTION FIVE

1

Slogan: **The End of Ceasefire**

A tableau of MAN-HSI *being sent to war. He stands at the centre.*

YU-LAI:

Glorious are those who volunteer
To throw down tyrants
March to the border when the millet sprouts
Fight for the people
Defend our homes and lands
Most glorious are the volunteers.

(MAN-HSI *goes to war. The village disperse, leaving* YU-LAI
with CHENG-K'UAN. HSIEN-E *is working in the house behind.*)

Slogan: **Civil War**

YU-LAI: What's wrong?

CHENG-K'UAN: Nothing.

YU-LAI: Don't look so sad, he's happy to go. He's been given land, and we'll farm it for him while he's away.

CHENG-K'UAN: Yes.

YU-LAI: Slut. Some soup. That's why we're going to win. Because our volunteers don't have to worry about their homes.

CHENG-K'UAN: The Kuomintang . . .

YU-LAI: *(Turning away)* If we can keep things on the move. (HSIEN-E *serves the soup.* T'IEN-MING *appears.)*

T'IEN-MING: There's a new directive . . .

YU-LAI: Good.

T'IEN-MING: From the Party.

CHENG-K'UAN: What does it say?

T'IEN-MING: It says if the war is to be won, the peasants must be mobilized. They must take over the land to win food to eat, clothes to wear, houses to live in. It says many peasants have still not fanshened.

YU-LAI: It's true.

T'IEN-MING: Serious feudal exploitation still exists.

YU-LAI: There are hundreds in the village who still don't have enough to make a living.

CHENG-K'UAN: How's it to be done?

T'IEN-MING: The land must be further redistributed.

CHENG-K'UAN: What land?

YU-LAI: We've scarcely begun. More soup.

CHENG-K'UAN: There aren't many gentry left in Long Bow. Two landlords, four rich peasants, it's not going to go very far.

YU-LAI: Middle peasants.

CHENG-K'UAN: You can start on the middle peasants certainly . . .

YU-LAI: Plenty of those.

CHENG-K'UAN: But if you take away their goods all you do is drive them over to the enemy side.

YU-LAI: That's a risk.

CHENG-K'UAN: The middle peasants already don't work as hard as they should, because if they work hard they become rich

31

peasants, and if they become rich peasants we take it all away. Like cutting chives.

YU-LAI: Does that matter?

CHENG-K'UAN: So the people in the village who can actually make a living, who can look after themselves, who ought to be our strength, will drift over to the Kuomintang.

YU-LAI: So what do you think we should do?

(He strikes HSIEN-E *who has returned with more soup.)*
You're an idle cunt.

(She goes.)
The whole village is convinced the Kuomintang will return. The Catholics openly plot our assassination, peasants have begun to creep back in the night to return the goods that were seized from landlords, grenades go off in the hillside, you ask about fanshen, people have never heard the word. We're at war. What do you think we should do?

(Silence.)
Leadership. Strong leadership, Cheng-k'uan. We must keep things moving.

CHENG-K'UAN: Well . . . *(A pause.)* What does the directive say?

T'IEN-MING: Cut off feudal tails. This time we must examine family history. Anyone whose father or grandfather exploited labour at any time in the past will have their wealth confiscated.

YU-LAI: Very good.

T'IEN-MING: We must go right back, right through the last three generations to look for any remaining trace of feudal exploitation.

YU-LAI: Very good.

T'IEN-MING: Cheng-k'uan?

(They look at CHENG-K'UAN. *Then* YU-LAI *goes up to him.)*

YU-LAI: If you don't beat down the drowning dog, he jumps up and bites your hand. *(Then he smiles and calls into the house:)* Slut. My Luger.

FANSHEN

(HSIEN-E *brings him his gun.*)
YU-LAI: And to work.

2

T'IEN-MING: The public meetings begin again. All the remaining members of families already under attack had their last wealth seized. And families with any history of exploitation were added to the list. With the enemy troops so close and counter-revolution so likely, the campaign was emotional and violent. When there was no more land to be had, we ripped open ancestral tombs, leaving gaping holes in the countryside. It looked as if the country had been bombarded with shells.

YU-LAI: But it was the living who bore the brunt of the attack. The gentry wives astonished us with their contempt for pain. We heated iron bars in the fire, but burning flesh held no terror for the women. They would die rather than tell you where their gold was hidden. They would only weaken, if at all, when their children were threatened.

CHENG-K'UAN: Slowly the advance of the Kuomintang was being halted. The military threat disappeared. And the campaign to find new wealth faded, a source of bitter disappointment to those of us who manned it. For when all the fruits had been divided, there were still many families who felt they had not fanshened.

3

HU HSUEH-CHEN *lying on the platform, her four-year-old daughter beside her.* T'IEN-MING *at the door carrying his possessions.*

T'IEN-MING: Hsueh-chen. Hsueh-chen.
(She wakes.)
I'm leaving tonight. Uh. Quiet, let me go quietly. I've been ordered to go and work at County Headquarters. You must elect a new secretary to the Party in Long Bow.
(Silence.)

33

Say nothing. I know what you're thinking. I can't help. One person doesn't make any difference. Hsueh-chen. I . . . two years ago I couldn't get a sentence out. The people . . . victory lies with the people.
(Silence.)
Good night.
(He goes.)

SECTION SIX

1
Slogan: **Nineteen Forty-eight**
A single man working in the field. As at the opening of SECTION ONE.
CHENG-K'UAN *on the tower.*
CHENG-K'UAN: There will be a meeting. There will be a meeting tonight.
(OLD TUI-CHIN *stops and looks up.*)
TUI-CHIN: Another meeting. Do the meetings never stop?
CHENG-K'UAN: Everyone to attend.
TUI-CHIN: 'Under the Nationalists too many taxes. Under the Communists, too many meetings.'
(He picks up an enormous pile of stubble, twice his own size and starts humping it home. He pauses. YU-LAI *sees him.)*
YU-LAI: Why aren't you at the meeting?
TUI-CHIN: They can meet without me tonight.
YU-LAI: Why?
TUI-CHIN: I'm busy. I'm tired.
YU-LAI: Come to the meeting.
TUI-CHIN: There's no point, there's nothing left to dig up, there's nothing. We'll just sit about and discuss redistributing our farts.
YU-LAI: Come to the meeting.
TUI-CHIN: Listen, we all struggled for this land. Now we're not given time to work it because we're at meetings talking about

34

where to find more land which even if we found it we wouldn't have time to farm because we're always at meetings.

YU-LAI: Come to the meeting.

TUI-CHIN: I haven't eaten.

YU-LAI: The meeting is for your own good. *(He hits him across the face.)* It's in your interest. *(He hits him again.)* You think I don't have my work cut out without chasing up idle cunts like you?

(TUI-CHIN *stumbles away.)*

Where do you think your fanshen came from, you lazy turd?

2

The work team. HOU, LITTLE LI, CH'I-YUN, CHANG CH'UER. *Platform.*

Slogan: **The Arrival Of The Work Team**

CH'I-YUN: We paused for a moment to look down into the valley. A long flat plain, in the centre a complex of adobe walls under a canopy of trees, the yellow fields stretching away on all sides. In the semi-darkness we could just see the last actions of the day: a donkey straining at a plough, a man raking corn stubble, a barefoot boy spreading night soil, a child playing with some sticks in a ditch. Over our heads the warm, motionless air hummed and whistled as a flight of swallows swooped low. The four of us stood a moment, none of us knowing each other, none of us knowing what to say. Then we began our descent into Long Bow.

(The work team enter the village.)

YU-LAI: *(Off)* You. Get out of that ditch and get to the meeting. *(Off.)* Is everyone in?

CHENG-K'UAN: *(Off)* All at the meeting.

(YU-LAI *appears, a broad smile on his face.)*

YU-LAI: Perhaps we should lock the doors.

(He looks up and sees the four of them standing looking at him.)

I don't know you.

FANSHEN

CH'I-YUN: Comrade.

HOU: I'm Hou Pao-pei, leader of the work team. We've been sent by the government to supervise land reform in Long Bow.

YU-LAI: I see. Wang Yu-lai, Vice-Chairman Peasants' Association.

HOU: Ch'i-Yun. Chang Ch'uer. Magistrate Li. Members of the work team.

YU-LAI: Welcome to Long Bow. *(Pause.)* We are all at a meeting, you've chosen a bad time.

LITTLE LI: Is there somewhere for us to stay?

YU-LAI: I'm sure.

HOU: We will be starting work at once.

YU-LAI: Yes?

HOU: Talking to the people, finding out how they've prospered . . .

CHANG CH'UER: Agricultural methods.

HOU: Yes.

CHANG CH'UER: Mutual aid schemes.

HOU: Examining the progress of the movement. Elsewhere there have been shortcomings. Some landlords, rich peasants, riffraff, have sneaked into the people's organizations, where they abuse their power, ride roughshod over the people and destroy the faith of the masses in their new organizations.

YU-LAI: You can sleep in the temple. I must go to the meeting. Mutual aid scheme. Discussion. You know.

(He looks at them, goes out. The four of them left standing.)

HOU: Good, excellent, very good. Right.

LITTLE LI: Do you . . .

HOU: Li, can you try and find the temple? We must know where we're going to sleep. *(He laughs.)*

LITTLE LI: Yes, of course.

HOU: Chang Ch'uer, perhaps you could help, Ch'i-Yun and I will go and . . . find the meeting. Is that best?

CHANG CH'UER: I think so.

LITTLE LI: Yes.

HOU: Good, then tomorrow we start meeting the people of the village. There's a lot to be done. Good luck.

(They scatter. CHANG CH'UER *remains.)*

CHANG CH'UER: The first day we watched each other, the four of us, unknown to each other, scrutinizing every reaction. The second day . . .

3

A man with a white scarf tied round his face runs on and strangles CHANG CH'UER. *They struggle for a long time. The man stuffs a towel down his mouth, then catches sight of* LAI-TZU *who is watching, a passer-by who happens to have caught the incident.*

The man runs off.

HU HSUEH-CHEN *runs out into the street.* HOU *appears.*

HOU: What's happened?

HSUEH-CHEN: This man . . .

HOU: It's Chang Ch'uer.

HSUEH-CHEN: Has been attacked.

HOU: Get a doctor.

LAI-TZU: It . . .

HSUEH-CHEN: There's no doctor in the village.

HOU: Where's the nearest?

LAI-TZU: Lucheng.

HOU: What's your name? Can you carry him to Lucheng?

LAI-TZU: I can find a stretcher. *(He goes out.)*

HOU: His pulse is very weak.

HSUEH-CHEN: Who is he?

HOU: He's a member of the work team. What's this?

HSUEH-CHEN: It's a towel.

HOU: It says ger oo de morenin. 'Good morning' in English.

(LAI-TZU *returns with the stretcher.*)

LAI-TZU: I heard the attack being plotted. A few hours ago. I know who did it.

(LITTLE LI *and* CH'I-YUN *arrive.*)

HOU: Chang Ch'uer has been attacked.

FANSHEN

CH'I-YUN: Is it the Kuomintang?

LAI-TZU: I overheard the planning.

HOU: Lift him carefully.

LAI-TZU: It was Wang Yu-lai.

HOU: Be careful. You're hurting him.

LITTLE LI: Yu-lai?

LAI-TZU: I overheard Yu-lai talking to his friends. I was listening . . .

LITTLE LI: Then why didn't you tell us?

HOU: Concentrate.

(They lift the body on to the stretcher.)

HOU: There.

LAI-TZU: Don't you want to know who did it?

HOU: I've heard what you say. Take him to Lucheng.

LAI-TZU: Do I get millet tickets?

HOU: Take him.

LAI-TZU: It's eight miles.

HOU: Little Li. Find someone who will take him.

(LITTLE LI *and* LAI-TZU *go off,* LAI-TZU *whining into the distance.)*

LAI-TZU: I'll take him, it just is a very long way, and if he were a wounded soldier, I'd be entitled to millet tickets, and I just want to know if the same thing applies to . . .

HOU: Is he trustworthy?

HSUEH-CHEN: No. He's a Catholic.

(A pause. HOU *screws the towel up.* CHENG-K'UAN *arrives.)*
Hu Hsueh-chen, I'm secretary of the Women's Association.

CHENG-K'UAN: Cheng-k'uan, chairman of the Peasants' Association.

HOU: You're both members of the Party, I know. Comrade Hou Pao-pei, leader of the work team.

HSUEH-CHEN: Welcome.

HOU: The man he accused . . .

HSUEH-CHEN: Yes . . .

HOU: Is a cadre in the Peasants' Association.

HSUEH-CHEN: He's Vice-Chairman.

HOU: Yes.

CHENG-K'UAN: And his son Wen-te is the Head of Police.

(Pause.)

HSUEH-CHEN: The towels are made by a co-operative in Hantan.

HOU: These?

HSUEH-CHEN: I've seen them in Yu-lai's home.

(LITTLE LI *returns.*)

LITTLE LI: The first day we arrive!

CH'I-YUN: Comrade.

HOU: Give me time to think. Just give me a moment.

LITTLE LI: If the leaders of the village take to attacking the work team . . .

HOU: Please. *(He turns to* HSUEH-CHEN.) Comrades. I am a peasant like you, I come from a village, not that many miles from here. I've lived the same life, so I think you'll understand what I do.

HSUEH-CHEN: Comrade.

LITTLE LI: I think we should . . .

HOU: Just . . . let me speak. I've only been here a few hours but already the work team has heard a good deal of complaint. Some people feel that fanshen is not complete. Some who feel they got too little, others who feel that the cadres took most. Whether this is true . . . an attack is made on the life of a member of the work team by a leader of the village on the first day we arrive to investigate.

(Pause.)

The Vice-Chairman of the Peasants' Association must be taken to jail. His son, Wen-te, the Head of Police, will be taken to jail. His closest friends must be arrested and taken to jail. The work team will be issued with guns. All village leaders are temporarily suspended. The Women's Association. The militia suspended. The village accounts will be examined by the work team. The Party branch will go into secret session to examine its own performance up till now. The work team will take over the affairs of the village. It will root out commandism, hedonism, opportunism. It will re-examine the whole village's fanshen.

(HSUEH-CHEN *is staring at* HOU.)

Comrades, I am not saying you . . . you are thinking of the hours you have all worked, of the days, of the months, of the years, you have given. Don't. Don't think of yourself. Think of the people and how they are led.

(HSUEH-CHEN *and* CHENG-K'UAN *go out, saying nothing.*)

Wipe the slate clean and start again. Is that not right, Little Li?

LITTLE LI: Yes.

HOU: Ch'i-Yun?

CH'I-YUN: Yes.

HOU: The place is rotten. We must start again.

SECTION SEVEN

1

LITTLE LI *addresses the poorest in the village.* LAI-TZU, TING-FU, YUAN-LUNG, HUAN-CH'AO, OLD LADY WANG, HSIN-AI, T'AO-YUAN. HOU *sits beside* LITTLE LI *as he speaks.*

Slogan: **The Draft Agrarian Law**

LITTLE LI: Brothers and sisters, peasants of Long Bow.

In the course of the past two years this region has carried out a powerful and enthusiastic land reform programme. Over ten million people have already fanshened. But there are some areas where the peasants have only partially fanshened or not fashened at all. Now finally everyone must fanshen.

In the past there were mistakes. There was favouritism. People got more because they were soldiers, or because they were cadres. Or because they were highly placed in the movement.

Now the Draft Agrarian Law will correct all such mistakes because it is firmly based on the slogan: 'Depend on the poor

40

FANSHEN

peasant, unite with the middle peasant, destroy the feudal system.'

Now what does this mean? It means the feudal system will be finally eliminated and replaced with a new system called 'Land to the Tiller'.

Lands and goods are to be redistributed on one basis and one basis only: how much you have now and how many there are in your family.

So no longer is it a question of what sort of person you are, of whether you are thought to have helped or hindered the movement. This time, those with merit will get some, those without merit will get some. All landlords' property will be divided and everyone will get a fair share. Now how is this to be done?

It is to be done by a rigorous process of classification.

Each head of family in Long Bow will be classified according to what he now has. If he is classified a poor peasant, or hired labourer, he will be given something. If he is classified a middle peasant, he will probably not be touched. If he is classified a rich peasant or landlord, he will have something taken away.

And this time it is you—the poor—the very poorest in the village, who will be in charge of the classification process.

You will run the meetings. Each family head must come before you and reveal his exact wealth and his exact needs.

You will discuss his report and decide his family's class status.

But beware. You—the basic elements—are holding a knife in your hands. We are at war. Class someone now as a rich peasant and he becomes your enemy. Class someone as a middle peasant and he becomes your ally. Class someone as a poor peasant and he becomes one of you. You must take care. For on these classifications will depend what everyone is to get, how they are to live for the rest of their lives.

(The peasants applaud.)

41

2

Slogan: **Self-report, Public Appraisal**

LAI-TZU: My name is Kuo Lai-tzu. I have two acres, there are four in my family. I have no children. I reap about ten bushels to the acre. And I don't have any kind of draft animals.

HOU: Discuss in groups.

(LAI-TZU *before the classification meeting. These are the poorest peasants again:* LAI-TZU, OLD LADY WANG, HUAN-CH'AO, T'AO-YUAN, TING-FU, YUAN-LUNG *and an old woman,* LI HSIN-AI. LI *and* HOU *are at the side, writing. The peasants are in distinct groups. The groups go into a huddle.*)

HOU: Report from your groups.

TING-FU: Poor peasant.

OLD LADY WANG: Poor peasant.

YUAN-LUNG: Poor peasant.

HOU: Poor peasant?

ALL: Yes, yes.

HSIN-AI: He hasn't even fanshened.

HOU: Poor peasant. I shall write it down. Next.

LAI-TZU: Told you.

(TING-FU *stands up.*)

TING-FU: Half an acre.

HOU: Name?

TING-FU: My name is Ting-fu. I have half an acre. No livestock, no implements. I have three sections of house.

YUAN-LUNG: Falling down.

TING-FU: And I share a privy, that's it.

OLD LADY WANG: Everyone knows him, he's a poor peasant.

LAI-TZU: He's the hardest worker in the village.

HOU: Poor peasant?

ALL: Yes, yes. Poor peasant.

HOU: Poor peasant. I shall write it down. Next.

(HUAN-CH'AO *steps up.*)

HUAN-CH'AO: My name is Chang Huan-ch'ao.

OLD LADY WANG: Yes well . . .

LITTLE LI: Let him speak.

HUAN-CH'AO: I'm a blacksmith. I have very little land because I don't farm. I have four sections of house. I have a family of four. That's all.

HOU: Discuss in groups.

OLD LADY WANG: There's no need. He's a middle peasant.

LITTLE LI: You must first discuss it in your group.

OLD LADY WANG: He's a middle peasant because he does so well out of everyone . . .

YUAN-LUNG: How . . .

OLD LADY WANG: His prices are high and his work's rotten.
(Laughter.)

TUI-CHIN: He's certainly a terrible blacksmith.

HOU: Please.

HUAN-CH'AO: No, go on. Say what you like, I'm very interested.

OLD LADY WANG: You . . .

HUAN-CH'AO: Very happy to hear what you think.

OLD LADY WANG: We think . . .

HUAN-CH'AO: Yes?

OLD LADY WANG: We think you're a disgraceful black-smith . . .

HUAN-CH'AO: I see, yes, that's very interesting.

OLD LADY WANG: And we wouldn't trust you to bang a nail up an elephant's arsehole.

HUAN-CH'AO: I see. Yes. That's very clear.
(Laughter.)

HOU: Listen, it doesn't matter what sort of a blacksmith he is . . .

LAI-TZU: It matters to us.

OLD LADY WANG: You said a middle peasant is someone who can make their own living . . .

HOU: That's not what I said. A middle peasant is someone who himself rarely labours for others. He does. He hires his labour to you. That makes him . . . *(He looks round for an answer.)*

TING-FU: A worker.

43

LAI-TZU: What's a worker?

HOU: I don't think . . .

YUAN-LUNG: He's a poor peasant.

OLD LADY WANG: If we say he's a poor peasant, he'll get something in the distribution and . . . I don't want him to get anything.

LITTLE LI: That really isn't . . .

OLD LADY WANG: If he were a good blacksmith I'd be happy for him to be a poor peasant.

HOU: Good and bad don't come into it.

YUAN-LUNG: Call him a poor peasant . . .

OLD LADY WANG: Who must improve his work.

HOU: You're a poor peasant who must improve your work.

LITTLE LI: Do we all agree?

TING-FU: No.

LITTLE LI: Why not?

TING-FU: He's a village worker.

LITTLE LI: We don't have that category.

TING-FU: Well, you should. We can't call him a peasant, peasants work on the land.

LITTLE LI: Well . . .

HOU: He's right.

TING-FU: You can't call him something he's not.

HOU: Thank you, Ting-fu. We'll think about it. Huan-ch'ao, we will defer your classification.

HUAN-CH'AO: Defer?

HOU: Yes. The next.

(HUAN-CH'AO *goes back to his seat.*)

HUAN-CH'AO: Just wait till it's your turn.

(T'AO-YUAN *steps up.*)

T'AO-YUAN: My name is Wang T'ao-yuan. Only two acres. No wife, no animals. My land was given me in the first distribution, two years ago. Before that I had no land at all. I have one nephew to support. That's all.

HOU: Discuss in groups.

(They do so. T'AO-YUAN *smiles broadly while he waits.)*
Each group to report.
(A representative stands up from each group.)

LAI-TZU: Our group wants to ask about the past.

HOU: Yes.

LAI-TZU: You used to have a lot of money.

T'AO-YUAN: I have had money, yes.

LAI-TZU: I mean, I can remember when you didn't work.

T'AO-YUAN: Well . . .

LAI-TZU: How did you live?

T'AO-YUAN: This and that.

LAI-TZU: You sold heroin.

T'AO-YUAN: I smoked it myself.

LAI-TZU: You sold it . . .

T'AO-YUAN: In a way.

LAI-TZU: What way?

T'AO-YUAN: Just to make money. I only sold it to make money.

LAI-TZU: Well why else . . .

HOU: All right.

(HOU *nods at the second group whose representative is* OLD LADY WANG.)

OLD LADY WANG: Tell us what happened to your wife.

T'AO-YUAN: *(To* HOU) Is this . . .

HOU: Yes.

T'AO-YUAN: Well . . . I began smoking heroin in the famine year and everything I had I spent on heroin. So when I had nothing left I took my wife to Taiyuan. I was very lucky, I managed to find a buyer quite quickly. He gave me six bags of millet, so that sealed the deal.

OLD LADY WANG: And other people's wives, you sold them?

T'AO-YUAN: I helped sell them, occasionally.

OLD LADY WANG: And you got paid for this . . .

T'AO-YUAN: I was usually given heroin.

OLD LADY WANG: So your income came either from selling heroin or selling other people's wives . . .

45

T'AO-YUAN: It's . . . one way of looking at it.

OLD LADY WANG: He should be classed as a landlord's running dog. *(She sits.)*

HOU: Next group.

HUAN-CH'AO: We want to ask about the donkey. You had a donkey?

T'AO-YUAN: Yes, I paid two hundred dollars for it.

HUAN-CH'AO: What happened to it?

T'AO-YUAN: It caught a cold, it died.

HUAN-CH'AO: I see. Thank you. *(He sits.)*

HOU: So.

OLD LADY WANG: May we ask what he now feels about selling his wife?

T'AO-YUAN: I feel . . . *(He begins to cry bitterly.)*

OLD LADY WANG: Really it was your own fault. You sold her and now you weep about it.

T'AO-YUAN: I'm not weeping for her. I'm weeping for my donkey.

(Silence.)

HOU: Classification. From your groups.

LAI-TZU: Middle peasant.

OLD LADY WANG: Rich peasant.

HUAN-CH'AO: Poor peasant.

(Silence.)

HOU: Discuss again.

3

LITTLE LI *working at a desk with a candle on papers.* HOU *is staring out into the fields.*

LITTLE LI: I have the results of the classification. Trying to make sense.

HOU: What is it?

LITTLE LI: One hundred and seventy-four families have been classed poor peasants.

HOU: Isn't that what we expected?

LITTLE LI: But only seventy-two have so far fanshened. It

means there are one hundred families in the village who barely scrape a living. And I've nothing to give them. We found one rich peasant. One. It's not going to go very far. *(Pause.)* It's not land, there's enough land, one acre for every man, woman and child in Long Bow. It's resources. Animals, carts, implements, houses. That's what we need.

HOU: I've been over the village accounts to try and see if anything was missed or stolen in the last distribution. Everyone says the cadres took too much, but I can't find anything. *(Pause.)*

LITTLE LI: So what do we do next?

HOU: Expand the Poor Peasants' League.

LITTLE LI: It won't create *things*, comrade. *(Pause.)* I was at college, many years ago. People used to say China is poor, it's poor because it lacks fertilizer, it lacks machinery, it lacks insecticides, it lacks medical care. I used to say no, China is poor because it is unjust. *(Pause. Then he smiles.)*

HOU: We must prove it, comrade.

LITTLE LI: Yes.

(The house lights come up.)

INTERVAL

ACT II

During the interval CHENG-K'UAN *and* HU HSUEH-CHEN *rehearse their speeches for the gate. You watch them prepare the words they will later deliver to the village.*

1

HOU *joins the cadres while* LITTLE LI *sets out the benches and tables.*

HOU: Are you ready?

CHENG-K'UAN: I'll never be ready. This is the most frightening day of my life.

HOU: Tell the truth and you have nothing to fear.

CHENG-K'UAN: I know that. But the people . . .

HOU: Trust them.

CHENG-K'UAN: I'd be happy to die tomorrow as long as I pass the gate.

(From outside the hall we hear the delegates shout 'Purify the Party'. They are YUAN-LUNG, LAI-TZU, HSIN-AI, HUAN-CH'AO *and* TING-FU. *They come in and are about to sit opposite the cadres when* HOU *begins to lead the singing of the Internationale. The cadres all join in.* HOU *knows it best. Then they sit down.)*

HOU: The Communist Party is the servant of the people. To prove to you how seriously we take our charge, we have publicly posted the names of our members. It is no longer a secret organization. Now its members will appear before you, the delegates of the people, they will criticize their past actions and invite your grievances. They will then ask you to judge their future suitability for office.

Slogan: **The Gate**

CHENG-K'UAN: Comrades, on behalf of the Party I welcome you, the delegates of the people, and hope that you will speak out clearly and fearlessly what you think. Certainly you need not fear any reprisal. In the past, you made me a cadre, but I am ready to admit that after fanshen I forget my poor friends. (YUAN-LUNG *gets up nervously to reply.*)

YUAN-LUNG: I am a poor peasant chosen as a delegate to help purify the Party. I hope every Party member will examine his past honestly. I cannot speak much. We are here because poor peasants do want to help the Party. So we can all fanshen thoroughly. *(He sits down, his ordeal over.)*

CHENG-K'UAN: So let me start. *(Pause.)* I was born in Long Bow but my family comes from Chih-chou. I grew up a Catholic, I was a hired labourer. I took part in struggle meetings as you know. Because of them I became Chairman of the Peasants' Association. This made me arrogant. For instance, when we had to collect tax grain we never talked it over with the people, we just met among ourselves and decided what each should give, then ordered people to hand over. I think this was wrong, it was obviously unfair. Also, I hit Tui-chin when he made a hurtful remark about my body, sheer bad temper and I have no excuse . . .

HSIN-AI: Tell us how much you won out of fanshen.

CHENG-K'UAN: Ah.

LAI-TZU: Yes.

CHENG-K'UAN: I won . . . more than the masses out of fanshen.

HSIN-AI: How much more?

CHENG-K'UAN: An acre of land. The best. Ten hundredweight of millet. And ten pieces of clothing. Good quality. *(Silence.)*
Then I joined the Party. I thought, I'm on the way up and nothing can stop me. I was working very hard and I thought

49

FANSHEN

what's the point of working hard if you don't get a little extra and live better than other people? It was wrong. It was wrong thinking. I've done so much that was wrong. I borrowed a pair of trousers from the public warehouse. They're worn out now. And I would like you to help me. I would like to hear your grievances.

(Pause.)

LAI-TZU: When you took the village tax grain to Hukuan . . .

CHENG-K'UAN: Yes.

(A known scandal.)

LAI-TZU: Tell us about that.

CHENG-K'UAN: It was last year. There were two of us, I was with An-ho. We claimed three dollars personal expenses. But in fact I spent the money on cigarettes.

LAI-TZU: Why did you do that?

CHENG-K'UAN: Why?

LAI-TZU: Why did you buy cigarettes?

CHENG-K'UAN: Because my thinking was wrong. I thought I'm a cadre, I'm allowed to loll about and smoke cigarettes. I'm willing to return the money.

HUAN-CH'AO: How much?

CHENG-K'UAN: All of it.

HSIN-AI: Why?

CHENG-K'UAN: Why? Because . . .

HSIN-AI: You said two of you spent the money.

CHENG-K'UAN: Yes.

HSIN-AI: So why promise to pay it all back yourself? It just proves you're insincere.

CHENG-K'UAN: Four of us spent the money.

HSIN-AI: Then say so.

HUAN-CH'AO: Tell the truth.

HSIN-AI: You don't have to take the blame for what other people did.

CHENG-K'UAN: No.

HSIN-AI: And don't just agree with us.

CHENG-K'UAN: No.

HSIN-AI: Being criticized doesn't mean saying yes to everything.

CHENG-K'UAN: Yes. No.

HSIN-AI: Be objective and then criticize yourself.

CHENG-K'UAN: Yes.

(Pause.)

YUAN-LUNG: The candlesticks.

HSIN-AI: Yes, the silver candlesticks that were seized from the church . . .

CHENG-K'UAN: Yes.

HSIN-AI: What happened to them?

CHENG-K'UAN: They were sold.

HUAN-CH'AO: What happened to the money?

CHENG-K'UAN: It was distributed, to everyone. It was among the fruits.

HSIN-AI: It was a fortune, they were silver candlesticks.

CHENG-K'UAN: I don't think it was that much.

HSIN-AI: Tell the truth.

CHENG-K'UAN: I really can't remember.

HSIN-AI: What do you mean you don't remember—we can find out.

CHENG-K'UAN: Yes.

HSIN-AI: We can ask the landlord's wife, Wang Kuei-ching was business manager for the church. We can ask her.

HUAN-CH'AO: Well?

CHENG-K'UAN: Ask her.

Slogan: **They Talked For Six Hours**

HOU: Are you ready with the list?

CHENG-K'UAN: All the accusations you have made today. I hit four of you. I failed to consult you. I gave random orders. I took two dollars. Some clothing. I can offer no explanation for the money from the candlesticks. I thought of myself and not of serving the masses. Do you have any further grievances against me?

(Pause.)

51

HOU: Then you must decide how to deal with him. Cheng-k'uan, you must leave.

CHENG-K'UAN: I have loved my family. And my home. Now I love . . . the Communist Party. I shall wait patiently for the decision of the masses.

(He goes out. A violent argument.)

HSIN-AI: Suspend him from the Party.

TUI-CHIN: Yes.

HSIN-AI: Send him to the People's Court in Lucheng.

YUAN-LUNG: Huan-ch'ao?

HUAN-CH'AO: I think . . . just make him give everything back.

LAI-TZU: I agree, he's admitted his mistakes . . . that's what we wanted.

HSIN-AI: How can he give everything back when he says he doesn't remember?

HUAN-CH'AO: Just give it back.

HSIN-AI: We suffered, now he must suffer.

TUI-CHIN: Send him to the Court.

HSIN-AI: He must understand pain.

YUAN-LUNG: Why not just ask him to jump down the well?

HSIN-AI: Why not? I don't care if he starves to death.

TUI-CHIN: The Party was meant to serve the people . . .

HSIN-AI: So long as he gives back what he got during fanshen.

TUI-CHIN: It was meant to lead us to fanshen. But in fact only members of the Party really fanshened . . .

LAI-TZU: Then take something away.

TUI-CHIN: They became officials, just like feudal officials . . .

LAI-TZU: And now he's sorry.

TUI-CHIN: Cheng-k'uan climbed on our heads . . .

HSIN-AI: They all did.

TUI-CHIN: And now we must throw him out.

LAI-TZU: You're talking about one of the most popular men in the village . . .

TUI-CHIN: That just shows you.

LAI-TZU: You're talking about two dollars . . .

TUI-CHIN: I'm talking about why, why our leaders are rich, why we're still poor . . .

LAI-TZU: The Party . . .

TUI-CHIN: The Party has asked the people to decide, and this is what we decide. Sent him to the Court.

HOU: The People's Court is for cases you cannot decide yourselves. Is that how you wish to be known? As the village that cannot decide the simplest case?

YUAN-LUNG: All we need to do is suspend him from office, just for a short time, and see if he really wants to reform.

TUI-CHIN: He should be thrown out of the Party.

YUAN-LUNG: No.

LAI-TZU: It was only two dollars . . .

TUI-CHIN: It's not what he did. It's what he let others do. How did Yu-lai come to rule this town?

(Pause.)

HOU: *(Very quiet)* Yu-lai is in prison.

TUI-CHIN: Yes. Because you came with guns. And threw him in prison. Good. But up till then . . . where were our leaders? Well?

(Pause.)

HOU: So. Do we agree? You suspend him and then see if he corrects his behaviour. Is that what you want?

ALL: Yes.

HSIN-AI: He should never be a cadre again.

HUAN-CH'AO: Be quiet, you old shitbag.

HSIN-AI: He should be thrashed with a dogwhip.

HOU: Listen. Because you've been beaten you want to see him beaten. All right. Now we oppose beatings and this makes you bitter. You think unless we flay the skin off his back, he'll just carry on as before. But that's feudal behaviour. We are living in a new society. Are we not?

(Pause.)

YUAN-LUNG: Suspend him from office?

ALL: Yes.

(LITTLE LI *goes to get* CHENG-K'UAN.)

53

HOU: For how long?

YUAN-LUNG: Six months?

ALL: Yes.

(CHENG-K'UAN *returns.*)

YUAN-LUNG: We have decided that you have failed the gate, and that you must be suspended from office. However, in six months you will be given another chance to pass.

CHENG-K'UAN: I am happy to accept the decision of the masses.

(CHENG-K'UAN *returns to his seat.* HSUEH-CHEN *rises.*)

HSUEH-CHEN: I was a beggar, then a Party member.

YUAN-LUNG: Who are you?

(He knows perfectly well. HSUEH-CHEN *smiles.)*

HSUEH-CHEN: Hu Hsueh-chen, Secretary of the suspended Women's Association. I was a beggar, then a Party member, then in the Associaton. I have always struggled for equality for women . . .

YUAN-LUNG: Just tell us what you did wrong.

HSUEH-CHEN: Yes.

YUAN-LUNG: We all know what you did right . . .

HSUEH-CHEN: Yes.

YUAN-LUNG: You're always telling us.

HSUEH-CHEN: Yes.

YUAN-LUNG: Outstanding revolutionary cadre. Some cretin even painted you on the wall. So stick to what you did wrong.

HSUEH-CHEN: I think you'll find I've done as you ask. I have a list here. I can name the twenty-three occasions when I feel I may have impeded the revolution.

YUAN-LUNG: We'd like them in alphabetical order.

HSUEH-CHEN: I believe until you make a list, you don't really know yourself. And if you don't know yourself you can't criticize yourself. And if you can't criticize yourself both privately and in front of the masses, you can't be a Communist.

(Quiet. The peasants all look at her, taking account.)

There is the occasion I shouted at Fa-liang. There is the occasion I called Chuan-e a whore and burnt her best dress because I thought it . . . unsuitable for a woman. There is the occasion I hit Tao-yuan for giving a girl heroin. There is the occasion I tried to get a meeting postponed so I could canvass . . .

HUAN-CH'AO: This is pointless.

HSUEH-CHEN: There is the occasion . . .

HUAN-CH'AO: It's pointless reading it out. We know it'll all be there, it'll all be listed, anything we can think of, but it won't . . .

HOU: What?

HUAN-CH'AO: It won't—it won't—it's not what she did, it's that —look on her face . . .

HSUEH-CHEN: Please . . .

HUAN-CH'AO: Of course she's got her list, it's perfect, but her face . . .

LAI-TZU: You can't blame a woman . . .

HUAN-CH'AO: Look at it, just look at it. She knows she's going to pass, that's what I can't bear, and it shows in her face.

HSUEH-CHEN: I promise you, I don't know.

HUAN-CH'AO: Look at you. All the time. I have suffered more than you. I know more than you. I'm a better person than you.

HSUEH-CHEN: I don't think that.

HUAN-CH'AO: Round the lips, just a slight turn at the side, and your head . . .

HOU: We can't pass or fail people's faces . . .

HUAN-CH'AO: Of course we can. That's just what we should do. Why does everyone bristle the moment she comes in? Because of that look that says she's a leader. That's why the people resent her.

HOU: Sit down.

(HUAN-CH'AO *sits.*
Pause.)

HOU: Hsueh-chen?

HSUEH-CHEN: I submit to the people. I will try to correct my face.

2

Slogan: **The Results Of The Gate**

COMRADE HOU *before the people of Long Bow.*

HOU: We have heard every accusation you have to make against your leaders. Twenty-six members of the Party have appeared before you. Twenty-two have passed the gate, four have failed. Four more still in jail after the attack on a member of the work team have not yet appeared. We have found fifty-five cases of beating. A hundred and three cases of personal selfishness and corrupt practice. Seventeen cases of illicit sexual relations of which half may be called rape. Eleven cases of forgetting one's class. We also found in spite of rumour that the cadres of Long Bow got very little more in fanshen than the people. Tomorrow the work team goes to a regional conference in Lucheng. I shall be able to tell the secretary how we have purged the Party of wrongdoing, and how you have begun the process of purification. I shall be able to say with pride: in Long Bow the Party submits to the People.

SECTION NINE

1

At once the tolling of an enormous temple bell. Underneath it sitting on a bench the work team in a row. Sober.

Slogan: **The Trip To Lucheng County**

An OFFICIAL *appears to usher them in.*

OFFICIAL: Secretary Ch'en will speak to the Long Bow delegation before the conference begins. He hasn't got very long. *(The* OFFICIAL *leads them through to where* CH'EN *is at his desk. The team are left standing.* CH'EN *shakes hands with* HOU.)

CH'EN: Comrade Hou. Good. Have you prepared your report?

HOU: Yes.

56

CH'EN: Good. It will be called . . . as soon as possible. For the moment, the matter of Yu-lai and his friends . . .

HOU: Yes.

CH'EN: Why was he arrested?

HOU: There was an attack . . .

CH'EN: I know.

HOU: On a member of the work team.

CH'EN: The arrest was a mistake.

(Silence.)

HOU: There was evidence . . .

CH'EN: I have heard rumours that the four cadres have been tried at a mass meeting and shot.

HOU: That's not true.

CH'EN: Of course not. The point is I have heard it, peasants throughout Lucheng County have heard it . . .

HOU: I can't . . .

CH'EN: Let me finish my point. Thirty miles away from Long Bow the rumours are credited. And they lend currency to the belief that the cadres were guilty. And that undermines the work of every cadre in the County. There was not enough evidence for an arrest.

HOU: There was a towel.

CH'EN: Saying 'good morning'. I know. My own towel says 'good morning'. I doubt if there is a village in all China that does not have twenty towels saying 'good morning'. *(Pause.)* You arrested them on the basis of rumour and suspicion. You had no firm evidence. The County police have already decided to release them. *(Pause.)* It seems you made your minds up about the village before you even got there. And then you accepted the worst version of everything you heard. Isn't it true you suspended all the cadres the very first day you were there? Isn't it true you put the whole Party branch under supervision and took control of the village yourselves? Isn't it true that by the second day you were publicly examining the village accounts before you commanded any support among the people? And from what I've heard of the Long Bow gate

57

you countenanced every slur the people could bring against their leaders. Cheng-k'uan failed the gate because he was suspected of misusing money from the sale of candlesticks.

HOU: Yes.

CH'EN: We've looked into that. The candlesticks weren't even silver. They were pewter. They were worth very little. And yet you went to Wang's widow for evidence, you went to a class enemy for testimony against a cadre. We have a name for what you did. We call it Left extremism. (CH'EN *picks up a document from his desk.*) Here is a report prepared by the third administrative district of the Taihang subregion. Your mistakes are already listed in that. You have sought support only from the poor peasants, thereby neglecting the middle peasants. You've treated Party members as if they were class enemies. Everything the poor peasants wanted you have believed and tried to give them. You have elevated their point of view to the status of a line. That line is in clear opposition to the official policy of the Party.

(Silence.)

I shall be using the work of your team as an example to the whole conference of Left deviation. I hope after criticism we shall be able to correct your faults.

(Silence.)

Shall we go in?

2

Among the ruins of a bell tower. Sitting by a ruined wall is CH'I-YUN *cooking soup.* LITTLE LI *appears quietly.*

CH'I-YUN: Is he still talking?

LITTLE LI: Secretary Ch'en? Yes. He's been talking four hours.

CH'I-YUN: What are we to do?

LITTLE LI: Work teams throughout the County are to return to their villages. The Secretary feels too many middle peasants have been pushed over to the enemy side. We need all the allies we can get. So he is introducing a new standard in classification. The line between the middle and the rich peasant is to be redefined. We must fix it precisely. It's harder. More complex.

(CHANG CH'UER *comes in, rubbing his hands.*)

CHANG CH'UER: Is there something to eat?

CH'I-YUN: Not yet.

CHANG CH'UER: I'm hungry. What were you talking about?

LITTLE LI: The new classification.

CHANG CH'UER: Ah yes. Classification.

(Silence.)

Why do you never talk about yourself, Little Li?

LITTLE LI: Mmmh.

CHANG CH'UER: We think about ourselves. All the time, we all do . . .

LITTLE LI: I . . .

CHANG CH'UER: I don't know why we always talk about the poor, the poor peasants. Here we are looking miserable as goats, and it's not because we're worried about the poor, it's because Secretary Ch'en has shat all over us.

CH'I-YUN: *(Smiles)* Yes.

CHANG CH'UER: Come on, cabbage. *(Pause.)* I really wouldn't mind being poor. It's a good life when you compare it with being a cadre.

(HOU *has appeared, confident.*)

HOU: You all heard the Secretary. I have details of the new system here. I don't think it should give us too much trouble. We shall go back to Long Bow tomorrow. What's for supper?

CHANG CH'UER: We can't go back.

(Pause.)

LITTLE LI: We must talk.

HOU: I think I should decide when we're to talk . . .

LITTLE LI: It's a warm night. Look at the stars. I suggest the form is self-criticism, yes?

HOU: I don't think . . .

CHANG CH'UER: Only if it's honest.

LITTLE LI: Of course.

CHANG CH'UER: From everybody.

HOU: What do you mean?

CHANG CH'UER: We can't go back till we've spoken.

(Pause. HOU *wanders away, serious now, to think what this means.* CH'I-YUN *speaks very quietly, regretful.)*

CH'I-YUN: You've lost the trust of your team. Sit down.

(Pause. HOU *sits.)*

HOU: Supper?

LITTLE LI: After. Criticism first. Ch'i-Yun?

CH'I-YUN: I think most of what Ch'en said is true. When I went to Long Bow I did think poverty was everything. I just looked for rags and fleabites, I thought the smellier the better; lice-ridden, shit-stained old men I thought wonderful, I can't get enough of it, I'm really doing the job. And I believed everything they said, every accusation made against the Party. That was wrong. I lacked objectivity.

(She looks round, handing it on like a baton.)

LITTLE LI: From the very start we persecuted the . . .

CHANG CH'UER: Criticize yourself.

LITTLE LI: From the very start I persecuted the village cadres. I was over-harsh, I assumed everything was true. I kept telling the village they were poor because the cadres had taken all the fruits. But really, how much did they take? And if it were all divided up, what difference would it make to the whole distribution? (LITTLE LI *looks at* CHANG CH'UER.)

CHANG CH'UER: For a long time I've been thinking mostly about myself. After I was attacked I was very ill, the medicine the doctor gave me was very expensive. So I asked my neighbours for help, but they just said, you're a cadre and cadres should serve the people like oxen. Now I'm away from home, from my wife, from my children, and no one is helping me in the mutual aid scheme while I'm away because they refuse to help cadres. All the time, all the time I'm thinking my land is rotting and the people do not trust their leaders . . . I'm a servant of the people but sometimes . . . I find the people very hard to like.

(CHANG CH'UER *looks up, the baton passed.* HOU *silent.)*

LITTLE LI: Comrade . . .

HOU: I'm not a good leader, I know that. I do try.

CHANG CH'UER: Honest, we said, honest.

HOU: I know I'm not clever . . .

CHANG CH'UER: We said honest. Not humble. Humble isn't honest. Humble's humble. Humble's a way of not being criticized . . .

HOU: I do try . . .

CHANG CH'UER: Whenever we've tried to criticize you, you just say I know it's terrible, I'm just such a terrible person, you say yes, yes I'm sorry of course I know I'm so weak . . . but that doesn't solve anything.

HOU: I lie awake at night . . .

CH'I-YUN: That's just what's wrong, don't you see? It's useless lying awake at night. It's no help to anyone, it's subjective. Your work style is undemocratic.

HOU: I thought this was to be self-criticism.

CHANG CH'UER: We can't go back if you won't talk to us.

HOU: I took the job on very proud, very confident, then I began to realize it was more difficult than anything I had done in my life. I lost my nerve.

CHANG CH'UER: Why didn't you . . .

LITTLE LI: *(Stops him)* Ah.

HOU: I became afraid to consult you. I felt Little Li was just waiting for me to put a foot wrong. I thought I must be strong or they'll think ill of me. That's what leaders always think. That's what leaders are. Do this. Do that. And at the back of the head . . . what do they think of me? *(He smiles.)* After Ch'en . . . after what Ch'en said to us today I realized I'm not suited to the job, I've led the team badly and I must resign.

CH'I-YUN: Oh no.

LITTLE LI: No.

CHANG CH'UER: Wrong, wrong, wrong.

LITTLE LI: Do you understand nothing?

CH'I-YUN: What rubbish.

LITTLE LI: 'I resign.'

HOU: I feel . . .

CHANG CH'UER: Always the hero, you . . . always want to be the hero. 'I resign.'

LITTLE LI: 'I resign.'

CHANG CH'UER: Wonderful.

HOU: I'm sure . . .

LITTLE LI: I? I? Who is this I? The I who said I don't want my decisions questioned?

(Silence.)

HOU: Yes. That I.

(Silence.)

CH'I-YUN: We have to go back tomorrow and set about reclassifying the village. It will not . . . go down well. No one will light fires for our return. We will have to explain, discuss, report, evaluate, classify, post results, then listen to appeals, explain again, discuss again, classify again, post revised results. How can we do it if we are thinking of ourselves?

(Silence.)

Right now we are thinking life is easier at home. But that is because we have been badly led.

HOU: I . . .

CH'I-YUN: Yes.

(Silence.)

Why do we live in this world? Is it just to eat and sleep and lead a worthless life? That is the landlord and rich peasant point of view. Enjoy life, waste food and clothes, have children. But a Communist works not only for his own life: he has offered everything to the service of his class. If he finds one poor brother suffering from hunger and cold, he has not done his duty. Comrade.

(Silence.)

You should talk to us more.

CHANG CH'UER: It doesn't solve my problem.

CH'I-YUN: Nothing will solve your problem.

CHANG CH'UER: Thank you.

CH'I-YUN: Except working harder.

CHANG CH'UER: I work eighteen hours a day.

CH'I-YUN: Work twenty. You can if you want to. If we make you want to. But Comrade Hou must give us a lead.

HOU: Yes.

(Silence. He is at the end of his personality.)

HOU: What should I do?

CH'I-YUN: You have just given us a totally inadequate account of your work as team leader. You must make specific accusations against yourself. Only then will we begin to get at the truth. Only then will we begin to work as a team. You must go back over every event. You must tell us how and where and when you went wrong. When you began not to trust us. You must trace back over everything, every detail, every bad thought.

HOU: Yes.

(Silence.)

I have led the team badly.

CH'I-YUN: Be specific.

HOU: Once . . .

SECTION TEN

1

Three different households.

TUI-CHIN *is sitting outside his house.* CHENG-K'UAN *is staring into a bucket containing a dead child. And in* WEN-TE's *house* HSIEN-E *is working. Meanwhile the work team try to go about their business.*

Slogan: **Yu-lai and Wen-te Return To Long Bow**

(YU-LAI *and* WEN-TE *walk down the village street,* TUI-CHIN *withdraws indoors and prepares to go to bed. As they look around . . .)*

YU-LAI: What is it?

WEN-TE: It's called chewing-gum. Someone gave me it in prison.

63

YU-LAI: Ah.

(WEN-TE *gives him the bit he has been chewing.* YU-LAI *puts it in.* CHANG CH'UER *goes to* TUI-CHIN'*s house.* YU-LAI *smiles at* WEN-TE.)

YU-LAI: What a place. Why did we return?

CHANG CH'UER: Comrade. There is a meeting tonight. Classification.

TUI-CHIN: I've been classified.

CHANG CH'UER: To help classify others.

TUI-CHIN: I have my own classification, that's enough. I'm tired and I'm going to bed.

CHANG CH'UER: Tui-chin.

TUI-CHIN: Don't raise your voice, I'll report you.

(YU-LAI *sits down outside the house and starts to polish his Luger.*)

YU-LAI: Go and find your wife.

(WEN-TE *goes into the house.*)

CHANG CH'UER: We need to form a new Peasants' League.

TUI-CHIN: We've got a Poor Peasants' League.

CHANG CH'UER: An official league this time, not a provisional.

TUI-CHIN: Ah.

CHANG CH'UER: To carry out a new classification, so we can form a Provisional Peasants' Association.

TUI-CHIN: We've got a Peasants' Association.

CHANG CH'UER: A new Peasants' Association . . .

TUI-CHIN: What for?

CHANG CH'UER: A new gate.

(Pause.)

TUI-CHIN: I'm tired.

(TUI-CHIN *turns away.* WEN-TE *faces* HSIEN-E *inside the house.* YU-LAI *still sits outside.*)

HSIEN-E: Wen-te.

YU-LAI: Tell her we're hungry.

WEN-TE: My father says we're hungry.

HSIEN-E: There's corn.

WEN-TE: She says there's corn.

YU-LAI: Rabbit. In a stew. With garlic. And leeks. Pork. Shrimp. Onions. Tell her. Dumplings with herbs. Beancurd. Tell her. Tell her to ask her friends in the village, tell her to visit their homes, suggest . . . they give us . . . their food.

(HSIEN-E *stares at* WEN-TE.)

HSIEN-E: There's some corn.

(WEN-TE *smashes* HSIEN-E *hard across the face. Then beats her.*)

TUI-CHIN: It's not as if anyone else'll be there . . .

CHANG CH'UER: That's not true.

TUI-CHIN: Nobody obeys orders here any more, what's the point?

CHANG CH'UER: Tui-chin.

TUI-CHIN: I was among the keenest, comrade. Among the first. Then when you came, you told us to denounce corrupt leaders. And I did. I denounced Yu-lai while he was in prison. And now he's been released. Do you think he doesn't know? Do you think he isn't waiting for revenge? Feel my back. I'm sweating.

CHANG CH'UER: We had no choice.

TUI-CHIN: At least before they would have killed him.

(*He prepares for bed.* CH'I-YUN *crosses to* CHENG-K'UAN's *house.* YU-LAI *calls to* WEN-TE *inside the house.*)

YU-LAI: What does she say?

WEN-TE: She says yes, certainly, at once, of course, she's just going, sorry to be so long, are you sure that's all you want? (WEN-TE *thrashes wildly at* HSIEN-E *with his belt. She runs out of the house, at great speed and away.*)

CH'I-YUN: Cheng-k'uan. Why is there no one at the meeting? Cheng-k'uan.

CHANG CH'UER: We will organize another gate. To bring Yu-lai and Wen-te before the people. Confront them with their crimes. Sort everything out. Will you testify? Will you denounce them before the gate?

TUI-CHIN: Yu-lai and Wen-te are innocent. Of everything. That's what I'll say.

(WEN-TE *comes out of the house. Stands beside his father.*)

WEN-TE: She's gone to get the food.

TUI-CHIN: I trusted you. We all did.

(YU-LAI *throws the chewing-gum to the ground.*)

YU-LAI: This stuff doesn't taste.

CH'I-YUN: I know it's hard. And it's tiring, Cheng-k'uan. But you must never give up.

CHENG-K'UAN: I buried the cord. I was told to bury the cord.

CHANG CH'UER: Are you coming to the meeting?

(Silence. CH'I-YUN *uncovers the child.)*

CHANG CH'UER: I promise, I promise to try and help.

CH'I-YUN: Tell me what happened.

CHENG-K'UAN: Our child was born in a wash-basin six days ago. None of us knew it was coming so it just fell into a dirty basin at my wife's feet. We had nothing to cut the cord. She was bent forward, the child was filthy, my wife couldn't move. At first I couldn't find the midwife. Then after an hour she came, with an old pair of scissors.

(Pause. CHANG CH'UER *leaves* TUI-CHIN'*s house.* TUI-CHIN *goes to bed.)*

CHENG-K'UAN: How can we go on? I'm tired. Everyone says I've fanshened, but what's changed? Where are the doctors? How I long for money. Doctors. Scalpels. Clothes, clean clothes.

CH'I-YUN: They'll come.

(CH'I-YUN *turns away.* YU-LAI *looks up smiling at* CHANG CH'UER.)

YU-LAI: What's the matter? Can't get anyone to your meetings?

CHANG CH'UER: They're frightened.

(Holding the gun with both hands at arms' length, YU-LAI *walks towards* CHANG CH'UER.)

YU-LAI: Use force.

CHANG CH'UER: They're frightened of you.

(YU-LAI *steps back. He is genuinely angry.* CH'I-YUN *has joined them outside.* YU-LAI *yells at the top of his lungs, red, demented.)*

66

YU-LAI: Has anyone. In the village. Any charge. Against me. Will anyone. Speak.

(A silence. Then YU-LAI *laughs and fires his gun in the air.* CH'I-YUN *turns away.* YU-LAI *looks up smiling at* CHANG CH'UER.)*

YU-LAI: Good night.

WEN-TE: Good night.

(They go into the house.)

CH'I-YUN: Until finally after many months a young bride led the way.

2

HSIEN-E *crosses the village at night.*

HSIEN-E: I'll give evidence at the gate.

CH'I-YUN: Hsien-e.

HSIEN-E: Against my father-in-law Yu-lai. And against my husband Wen-te.

CH'I-YUN: Let me light this lamp.

HSIEN-E: No. If I testify . . .

CH'I-YUN: Yes.

HSIEN-E: I must never see him again. They'd kill me.

CH'I-YUN: Yes.

HSIEN-E: And I shall want a divorce.

(Pause.)

CH'I-YUN: You must go to the County . . .

HSIEN-E: I know. But first I must have the backing of the Women's Association, you must promise me that . . .

CH'I-YUN: No one has ever been divorced in Long Bow, the men will be against it . . .

HSIEN-E: Of course.

CH'I-YUN: And the older women.

HSIEN-E: Wen-te beat me. And Yu-lai. With a mule-whip. Often to within an inch of my life. I must have the backing of the Associaton. If I am not given a divorce, I will kill myself. *(Pause.)* What do you say?

CH'I-YUN: I say, come in, sleep here, never go home again. We will look after you. Plead your case to the Women's Association, then appear at the gate. I say that women . . . are half of China.

(The banner unfurls to read Women Are Half Of China. *An embrace. The scene breaks.)*

3

HOU: To bring before the gate those who have so far avoided it.

Slogan: **The Second Gate**

(This gate is in the church. Present are WEN-TE, HSIEN-E *and* YU-LAI. *At the side are* COMRADE HOU *and* LITTLE LI. *Delegates to the gate are* TUI-CHIN, CHENG-K'UAN, HSIN-AI *and* HUAN-CH'AO.)

HOU: Wang Wen-te, son to Wang Yu-lai, suspended Head of Police. You must criticize yourself.

WEN-TE: I don't want to . . . everything. I'll just list the things. I once beat Hsi-le because he was moaning about fanshen, saying it had been a mistake, so I rapped him about the face a couple of times. That was wrong, I should have talked to him. Also, bitterness. I admit to cursing the work team, when they sent me wrongfully to prison. In public I called them cunts. I said . . . Comrade Hou was a cunt. That was wrong. Also . . .

*(*YU-LAI *comes into the meeting late. Walks down the aisle. Sits down. Everyone watches him.)*

WEN-TE: I once . . . gave Huan-ch'ao a thrashing because of some silly gossip.

HUAN-CH'AO: It wasn't gossip, it was true.

HOU: Let him speak.

WEN-TE: I know that was wrong.

HUAN-CH'AO: Why did you beat me?

HOU: Let him finish.

WEN-TE: I think that's all. I don't think anybody here would have . . . any serious things to add. I would be surprised.

(He looks at them all daring them to speak. HUAN-CH'AO *rises and goes right up to him.)*

HUAN-CH'AO: Turtle's egg. Donkey's tool. Your mother's stinking cunt. *(He puts a finger in his face and shouts.)* You beat me because I told the truth. I said you beat your wife. That's why you left me for dead. Because I told the truth.
(He tries to strangle him. HOU *separates them.)*
HOU: Get him off. Get him off.
HUAN-CH'AO: *(Screaming)* I was left for dead. *(He is dragged off. Then looks round.)* Why? Why have you stopped me? Am I the only one? Am I the only man in Long Bow? I risk my life to accuse them. And you . . . when you find my body in a ditch, you will know everything.
(He sits down. YU-LAI *speaks very quietly.)*
YU-LAI: The man is mad. There's no case to answer.
*(HSIEN-E *stands at once. Her assurance and command are stunning.)*
WEN-TE: Not her.
HSIEN-E: When I was ten, my parents were starving, they sold me to be engaged to Wen-te. In return they got grain and money. I had to go and live in Yu-lai's home. He starved me, I had to go into the fields to find herbs to stay alive. They gave me only water. When I was fourteen, they made me marry him. After the marriage they often locked me in the house for weeks. Wen-te locked the doors and whipped me with a mule-whip. His father was free with me. I have made up my mind to divorce him, I have the backing of the Women's Association. Have I said enough?
HOU: Did you beat her?
*(WEN-TE *looks at* YU-LAI. YU-LAI *almost nods.)*
WEN-TE: Once or twice.
HOU: Why?
YU-LAI: Because she used to flirt in the cornfield, with other men. She was late with supper because she'd been whoring . . .
*(TUI-CHIN *like a barrack-room lawyer.)*
TUI-CHIN: How old was your wife when you married her?
WEN-TE: She . . .

69

HSIEN-E: Fourteen.

WEN-TE: Fifteen.

YU-LAI: Sixteen.

WEN-TE: Sixteen.

TUI-CHIN: How did you get a licence at the district office?

HSIEN-E: He ordered me to say I was sixteen.

TUI-CHIN: Is that true? *(Pause.)* Is that true? *(He turns to* HSIEN-E.*)* Why did you agree to lie?

WEN-TE: Because she wanted to marry me of course.

TUI-CHIN: Then you admit she lied. *(Pause.)* Why did you agree?

HSIEN-E: Because they threatened my parents.

TUI-CHIN: How?

HSIEN-E: They threatened to denounce them as Kuomintang agents.

HUAN-CH'AO: Anyone who disobeyed them was called a spy.

HSIN-AI: Yes, that's how they dealt with everyone.

HOU: What do you say?

WEN-TE: It's . . . very hard to remember. I can't remember. I can't remember the answers. *(Pause.)* Criticize me. While I try to remember the answers.

Slogan: **They Talked For Eight Hours**

(Change of pitch. WEN-TE *is broken, muttering inaudibly.* YU-LAI *is frozen, a Buddha. The pace is furious.)*

TUI-CHIN: The opinions of the masses pile up like a mountain.

CHENG-K'UAN: The list of charges is now five foot long.

WEN-TE: I can't remember anything.

TUI-CHIN: He doesn't understand, he doesn't even know what's going on. *(He is delighted.)*

WEN-TE: Criticize me. Please.

HSIN-AI: Kick him out of the Party and send him to the County Court.

ALL: Yes.

HOU: Do you agree to that, Wen-te?

WEN-TE: Of course. Yes. Send me to the Court. I deserve it. I have betrayed the masses.

HSIEN-E: And will you grant me a divorce?
(He looks up at her. Then bursts into a fit, banging his head on the ground on each 'Never'.)
WEN-TE: Never. I will never agree to that until the last minute of my life. Never. Never. Never.
HSIEN-E: You must.
WEN-TE: I will never beat you again.
HSIEN-E: He's lying.
WEN-TE: Never.
HSIEN-E: What if you beat me to death?
WEN-TE: I take an oath before the people.
HOU: *(Quiet)* That's enough, Hsien-e. He won't give you a divorce.
HSIEN-E: But . . .
HOU: We can't help.
(Silence. She sits down.)
The case demands . . . the severest punishment. Party members have a trust which you have betrayed. The people say you must go to the County Court.
(YU-LAI gets up, his patience exhausted.)
YU-LAI: Bonehead. Plank. Donkey's anus. I coached you for three days and you didn't get one answer right.
(WEN-TE begins to cry.)
HOU: Next before the gate. Wang Yu-lai.
(The people look glad.
Three tableaux of accusation. Then he is thrown down in the cadres' office by LITTLE LI. The rest scatter.)

4

LITTLE LI: You'll sleep in here. We'll keep you here until your trial.
YU-LAI: I want to die. I want to be left to die. There's nothing. Going back to prison, there's nothing.
LITTLE LI: You have betrayed the people. And you have failed the gate. There should be nothing.
YU-LAI: What can I do?

LITTLE LI: You should have told the truth, then you would have had some chance.

YU-LAI: If I'd told the truth they would have killed me.

(Enter CHANG CH'UER *and* CH'I-YUN, *very up.)*

CH'I-YUN: Where is he?

CHANG CH'UER: The people are cheering. The people have just cheered us through the streets.

CH'I-YUN: There's a celebration tonight.

CHANG CH'UER: The work we can do.

(COMRADE HOU *comes in with* SECRETARY LIU.)

HOU: Secretary Liu, this is the man. Members of the work team, this is Secretary Liu. He has come from Taihang to check on the progress of the work.

LITTLE LI: Comrade.

CH'I-YUN: Comrade.

LIU: Why is he crying? *(Pause.)* Tell me why you are crying.

YU-LAI: I want to die.

LIU: Why?

YU-LAI: There's nothing.

LIU: Nothing?

YU-LAI: Nothing for me.

LIU: Why?

YU-LAI: If I'm sent to the People's Court, I'll be shot.

LIU: Who told you that?

YU-LAI: If I confess everything, I'll be lynched. Or they'll throw me out of the Party and that's as bad as being shot.

LIU: Yes.

YU-LAI: People hate me, they want me dead.

LIU: You can still decide your fate. It's up to you. I know people who have done much worse than you. They have faced the people honestly and the people have accepted them again as leaders.

YU-LAI: I can't face living in this . . .

LIU: You can. Everyone can face everything.

YU-LAI: The people hate me.

LIU: No. They hate what you've done. *(Pause.)* The people have

72

voted to send you to the Court. You are not yet in prison. Walk down the street. Try it.

(YU-LAI *goes.*)

How did this happen? You let him lose hope. How could you? Never, never let a man lose hope. It's a waste, to the Party. To the people. It's easy, it's so easy to stamp something out. It's what they do in every country in the world. They cure diseases by killing the patient. But we . . . are going to save the patient.

CHANG CH'UER: You're going to let him loose?

LIU: Why not?

LITTLE LI: He and his son terrorized the village . . .

LIU: Ah I see so you thought get them out of the way and everything will be all right . . .

LITTLE LI: The people . . .

LIU: But it won't, comrade. You can't smooth trouble over, it will come back at you, always it will appear somewhere else unless you dig out the root.

CH'I-YUN: The people wanted rid of him.

LIU: Of course . . .

LITTLE LI: And we proved, we proved today we could remove their fears . . .

LIU: Of course you did, that's the easy part . . .

LITTLE LI: We proved today the Party is ready to purify its own ranks . . .

LIU: No. You proved the Party could be brutal and wasteful. There is a school in Changchih for cadres who cannot pass the gate. A place where they can be re-educated, taken out of their own lives, given a chance to think, to learn, to be objective. He should go there. He should not go to prison. On no account should he be thrown out of the Party. (*Pause.*) It's a practical question, you must say what you think.

CHANG CH'UER: Send him to the school. We can use him.

HOU: Yes. Our thinking was wrong.

CH'I-YUN: Yes.

LITTLE LI: No. We said purify the Party, we promised that. Now we mustn't go back. The people need to see him punished.

LIU: Or is it you who needs that?

LITTLE LI: We worked so hard to organize that meeting.

LIU: And you want a reward?

LITTLE LI: I want justice.

LIU: Well?

HOU: The overall feeling of the team is strongly for reforming the man.

LIU: Good.

LITTLE LI: If men like Yu-lai can remain as Communists then what is the point of the campaign?

LIU: There are no breakthroughs in our work. There is no 'just do this one thing and we will be there'. There is only the patient, daily work of re-making people. Over each hill, another hill. Over that hill, a mountain. The Party needs Yu-lai because he is clever and strong, and reformed will be of more value to the people than if he had never been corrupted. We must save him. We can use him. He can be reformed.

SECTION ELEVEN

1

SECRETARY CH'EN *addresses the delegates from the platform.*
Slogan: **The Second Lucheng Conference**

CH'EN: Comrades. The twenty-year war is almost over. Chiang Kai-shek's armies are doomed. A People's Republic is within our reach. And so we have come to a turning point. And we have called you in today because many wrong ideas have been shared and many wrong actions have been taken.

At our last meeting in Lucheng you were told that land reform was far from complete. We have now discovered, after surveys of the area, that this was wrong, that the feudal system in our County has been fundamentally abolished. The peasants have in the main fanshened. The surveys show that in Lucheng County the poor peasants now farm an average of four-fifths of an acre each, the middle peasants slightly less, the rich peasants one-sixth of an acre each. So there is only one land problem remaining and it is the very opposite of what you imagine: the attack has been overdone.

Think back all of you to the Draft Agrarian Law. Think back to Article 16. 'In places where the land has already been distributed before the announcement of the law, the land need not be further redistributed.'

Is this not such a place? Had we not already spontaneously and in advance of the Party undertaken land reform at the end of the Japanese occupation, BEFORE the law was announced?

Work teams have been applying land reform policy long after land reform has occurred. Because some people still have less, work teams have continued to hunt for non-existent wealth. They have continued to blame and persecute old rank-and-file cadres. And they have frightened and alienated many middle peasants, men who were never exploiters but who have always been our allies, and should have been treated as such.

Now how did this wrong line come about? It came about through an excess of zeal. It came about through blind utopianism, because so many work teams were ensnared by the idea of equality, of wanting to give everybody in China equal shares. This idea is dangerous. It encourages wrong standards. It has been condemned by Marx, by Engels, by Lenin, by Stalin. It is Leftism.

Equality cannot be established by decree. Even if we could give everyone an equal share, how long would it last? The strong, the ruthless would soon climb to the top; the weak and the sick would sink to the bottom. Only in the future when all land and productive wealth is finally held in common and we produce in great abundance will equality be possible.

So we have been judging fanshen by the wrong principles. We have taken absolute equality as our banner. We have

tried to be charitable. We have tried to give everyone everything they need. We have tried to be god.

Land reform can have only one standard and it is not equality. It is the abolition of the feudal system. And that we have
achieved.

Now we know from history that whenever victory draws
near it's easy for cadres to become adventurist, to alienate
their allies, to persecute creators of wealth, to make impossible leftist demands. This is counter-revolutionary, because it
pits working people against working people and endangers
the success of the whole movement.

We must rein ourselves in. Above all in Lucheng County we
must begin the work of returning goods and land to those
middle peasants from whom we have taken too much.

And we must ensure that landlords are given enough land
to make a living.

(LITTLE LI *gets up and leaves.*)

How this is to be done we shall discuss in the coming days.

2

LITTLE LI *pacing up and down in the square is joined by the rest
of the work team.*

LITTLE LI: It's insane. It's totally insane.

HOU: Li . . .

LITTLE LI: The policy has changed again.

Slogan: **They Talked For Sixteen Hours**

LITTLE LI: We are to go back to the village, we are to tell the
people Article 16 has been overlooked, this means the fanshen was finished two years ago, you've had all you're going to
get, in fact you're going to have to give some back.

CH'I-YUN: You're frightened of the people, Little Li. Frightened to admit you made a mistake.

LITTLE LI: I didn't make it. He did.

CH'I-YUN: Who?

LITTLE LI: Ch'en.

HOU: Then tell him.

LITTLE LI: They just change the policy whenever it suits them.

HOU: I shall go and find Secretary Ch'en and tell him the Long Bow delegation wishes to speak to him.

LITTLE LI: Don't be ridiculous. He won't even come.

HOU: I shall tell him you have a criticism. I've no doubt he'll come. *(He goes out.)*

LITTLE LI: If the Party can make mistakes like that, what is there for us to cling to?

CHANG CH'UER: I don't feel that. I feel as if a great rock has been lifted from my back. These last few months I'd come to feel a fool, thrashing around for wealth, trying to level people out, pushing people about. I felt tired and resentful and angry. And now I see my political thinking was wrong, I took a wrong line, I had the wrong objectives, and far from feeling bitter or betrayed, I just feel . . . the knot is untied and I can look at the very same village, the very same people, I can look at the very same facts and I feel happy and hopeful.

(A silence. Then noiselessly HOU *returns with* CH'EN.*)*

CH'EN: You wanted to see me.

LITTLE LI: Yes. *(Pause.)* I felt . . . the policy had changed.

CH'EN: No.

LITTLE LI: You changed the policy.

CH'EN: No. *(Pause.)* The policy has always been the same. 'Depend on the poor peasants, unite with the middle peasants, destroy the feudal system.' That has always been the policy, is still the policy, and will be the policy in places where the feudal system has not been uprooted. Here it has been uprooted. That we got wrong.

LITTLE LI: We?

CH'EN: That we got wrong.

LITTLE LI: We? We didn't get it wrong. You got it wrong. *(Silence.)*

You got it wrong. I want to hear you say 'I take the blame.' *(Pause.)* Last time we were here you criticized us for arresting Yu-lai. But it was you who approved the arrest in the first place. *(Pause.)* Say the words 'I take the blame.'

CH'EN: Each level of leaders does its best to understand overall policy and apply it locally. If you are given a theory you must test it in practice. If it fails in practice it is up to you to send it back. Everyone must be active. Everyone must think all the time.

LITTLE LI: 'I take the blame.' Say it.

(Pause.)

CH'EN: Primary responsibility for this last mistake rests with us at County headquarters. I take the blame.

(Silence.)

LITTLE LI: You're just saying it.

(CH'EN *raises his hands.)*

LITTLE LI: You're just saying it to get me back to work.

HOU: Li, you're behaving like a child.

CH'EN: It's not relevant.

LITTLE LI: I thought it was justice, I thought we were interested in justice.

CH'EN: Not as an abstract, as a practical thing. We've done what we can. From now on everyone's improvement must depend on production, on their new land, their new tools. If we'd gone on trying to equalize we'd have destroyed even that. Land reform can't be a final solution to men's problems. Land reform is just a step opening the way to socialism. And socialism itself is transitional. All we've done these past few years is give as many people as possible land to work. But our political choices have still to be made. Is each man now to work for himself? Is the pistol fired and the race underway, everyone climbing on each other's back? Or are we to build mutual aid, exchange labour, create property in common, hold the land collectively so we can all prosper together? You see the question has barely been asked. We haven't begun. *(Pause.)* You must go back.

HOU: Yes.

CH'EN: You must explain our mistakes, the people will be perfectly happy to listen. Tell the people the truth and they will

78

FANSHEN

trust you. One day, some time, this is the hardest thing, they will tell you the truth in return.

Tell them why China must be bold in concept but gentle in execution. Tell them . . . they are makers of the revolution every one.

They have lived already through many mistakes, but these are just ripples on the surface of the broad yellow river. Go back. Tell them.

SECTION TWELVE

1

A musical note, low, sustained.
Village life. Dawn. The village at work. The work team return.
They look about the village. People hoeing.
They begin to stop people one by one. Simultaneous dialogue based on the following in each different part of the stage.
You're going to have to give back . . .
Give back?
Yes, it's difficult to explain, let me explain, let me try to explain, there are good reasons.
(and)
I'm afraid there's been a change of policy. We've been to Lucheng.
I see.
It's best to tell you. I'd like to tell you . . .
(and)
We think it's best if you know exactly what's happening, there's been a change of policy.
Yes.
A good change, I think, but it sounds . . . hard on the surface anyway let me explain.
(and)
I'd like to explain to you what happened at Lucheng and then you tell me what you think. It'll need some thinking about.

79

FANSHEN

(As they talk the musical note turns into a superb massive groundswell of music that consumes the stage. Banners flood down so that the whole stage is surrounded in red. At the centre the cadres mutter on, gesturing, explaining, trying to hold the peasants' attention, getting a variety of first responses. Just before they are drowned out each cadre gets to the question:)
I'd like to know what you think.
Tell me.
Let me know what you think.
What do you think about this?
(Then they drown in sound and light.)

2

A single peasant. Hoeing in the field, as at the beginning. HOU *boxes the compass from the tower: 'There will be a meeting.'*
PEASANT:
There is no Jade Emperor in heaven
There is no Dragon King on earth
I am the Jade Emperor
I am the Dragon King
Make way for me you hills and
    mountains
I'm coming.
(He goes to the meeting. The banner round the theatre unfurls the words of the poem.)

SAIGON
Year of the Cat

For Lewis, my son

CHARACTERS

At the Bank:
BARBARA DEAN
MR HALIWELL
QUOC
DONALD HENDERSON
LHAN
PHU
Tellers, Customers etc.

At the Embassy:
BOB CHESNEAU
JACK OCKHAM
FRANK JUDD
JOAN MACKINTOSH
COLONEL FIEDLER
LINDA
THE AMBASSADOR
Secretaries, Officers, GIs etc.

Elsewhere:
VAN TRANG
NHIEU
BRAD
BARBARA'S MAID
Waiters, Bar Girls, People of Saigon

Saigon: Year of the Cat was first shown on Thames Television in
November 1983. The principal parts were played as follows:

BARBARA DEAN	Judi Dench
BOB CHESNEAU	Frederic Forrest
QUOC	Pitchit Bulkul
THE AMBASSADOR	E. G. Marshall
JACK OCKHAM	Josef Sommer
FRANK JUDD	Wallace Shawn
DONALD HENDERSON	Roger Rees
MR HALIWELL	Chic Murray
COLONEL FIEDLER	Manning Redwood
JOAN MACKINTOSH	Thomasine Heiner
NHIEU	Po Pau Pee
PRESIDENT THIEU	Thavisakdi Srimuang
Director	Stephen Frears
Producers	Verity Lambert
	Michael Dunlop

PART ONE

1. INT. LIVING ROOM. DAY

We are tracking through Barbara's apartment in the largely diplomatic section of Saigon. The blinds are all down against the fierce sun outside. It is dark and quiet and looks cool. There is a little plain furniture in good taste. The living room is bare-floored, tidy, the chairs in plain wood with white cushions. As we move through, we hear BARBARA's *voice.*

BARBARA: *(Voice Over)* Afternoons have always hit me the hardest, I don't know why that is, it's always been so. . . .

2. INT. BEDROOM. DAY

Into the bedroom, continuous, past the door jamb. We can make out very little, except slits of light across blinds at the end of the room. There is a dim lamp on beside a double bed on which BARBARA *lies. We track nearer.*

BARBARA: *(VO)* Mornings are fine, there's something to look forward to, and evenings, yes, I begin to cheer up. . . .

(In the bed BARBARA *is lying bunched sideways, not really reading the paperback in her hand. She is in a cream slip, covered by a sheet. She is almost 50 and blonde. She has the quietness and reserve of the genteel English middle class, but in her it has a pleasantness which is definitely erotic. She is sweating slightly as we approach.)*

(VO) But what would I wish for if I could wish for anything? This would be my wish: abolish afternoons.

3. EXT. TU DO. DAY

Later. After her siesta, BARBARA *in a linen dress walking down the busy street at the centre of Saigon. Shops, cyclists, the low blue taxis. The Vietnamese selling food and American PX goods on the sidewalk.*

BARBARA: *(VO)* It was never my intention my life should be secretive, it came about by accident, I think. . . .

(She goes into a small newsagent's.)

My first affair was with a friend of my father's, so really the style was adopted from then.

(She reappears with the airmail edition of The Times, *and walks on down the street.)*

People say, 'Barbara, I've never known anyone so secretive.' But it's only something which has happened with the years.

4. INT. HALIWELL'S OFFICE. EVENING

A Victorian-seeming office with a fan above. HALIWELL *working at a mahogany desk. Behind him, a large old-fashioned safe and wooden filing cabinets. He is in his late fifties with some silver hair left. A bachelor, fattening slightly, in a cotton shirt.*

BARBARA: Mr Haliwell.

HALIWELL: Barbara. A satisfactory siesta?

BARBARA: Fine. I collected the paper.

HALIWELL: Ah thanks.

(He looks up. A routine.)

Any news of the Arsenal?

BARBARA: I haven't looked. The sport's on page ten.

5. INT. BANK. EVENING

An old-fashioned commerical bank. Busy. Vaulted ceilings. Grandeur. Fans. The Vietnamese sitting behind iron grilles, serving a clientele of Asians and whites. Beyond the grilles, a large open area where the desks of the more senior staff are set out. A CLIENT *is being ushered in to meet* BARBARA *by* QUOC, *a tall, thin, grave Vietnamese in his late forties, who wears grey flannel trousers and a short-sleeved shirt. The client is named* TRINH.

BARBARA: Hello.

(She shakes TRINH's *hand and gestures him to sit opposite*

her. QUOC *brings round documents to her side of the desk and puts them down.)*
Mr Quoc has explained your application. You have good collateral.

TRINH: Yes.

BARBARA: You're securing the loan with the rest of your cargo fleet?

QUOC: Mr Trinh has fifty ships between here and Punan.
(QUOC has confirmed this by discreetly referring to a paper which BARBARA has in the file in front of her. She smiles warmly at TRINH and begins to write on the file.)

BARBARA: In that case I can't see there'll be any problem.

QUOC: *(Discreetly again, on TRINH's behalf)* Mr Trinh is only worried about time. How long we may give him for repayment.

BARBARA: *(Quietly, not looking up)* I'm not giving anyone more than a year.

6. INT. BANK. EVENING
The bank now deserted, BARBARA *tidying her desk. Beyond her the door to Haliwell's office is open and* HENDERSON *is packing away the contents of the safe for the night. He is a young Scot about 25, with a beard, very lean. He is talking from the other room.*

HENDERSON: That's the bastard of supporting St Mirren, they don't always have the result in *The Times.*
(BARBARA gets up to go.)
It's Scotland who go on producing the players, but when you look for coverage, it's Leeds, Leeds, Leeds. I mean, it's ridiculous, they're all Scottish players . . .

BARBARA: Yes, it's tricky I see.

HENDERSON: That and economic misfortune. It's barely worth reading the thing any more.
(She has gone to the main door and is about to open it to leave. HENDERSON *has appeared at the door of Haliwell's office. He speaks from right across the bank.)*

Barbara . . .

BARBARA: Yes?

HENDERSON: Are you free for this evening? I was hoping we'd be able to go out. It's been some time.

(There's a pause. He looks down, a little embarrassed. Then with some personal feeling:)

It was wonderful last time.

(She looks at him, straight across the bank, her manners perfect.)

BARBARA: Oh Donald, I'm sorry. I'm busy tonight.

7. INT. CERCLE SPORTIF. NIGHT

The main lounge of the Cercle Sportif. A French colonial club. A large central room, bamboo armchairs, white-coated servants with trays. BARBARA *stands at the main entrance, dressed smartly but lightly for the evening.* FRANK JUDD, *a fat, bespectacled 32-year-old American in seersuckers and short-sleeved shirt, moves across at once to greet her.*

JUDD: Barbara. Hi.

BARBARA: Frank. How are you?

JUDD: Come and meet the rest.

(They have arrived next to two men who are sitting drinking. They now stand up. COLONEL FIEDLER *is a powerfully built American army officer of 55, in uniform.* VAN TRANG *is a small fat Vietnamese of the same age, in a shiny black suit.)*

Barbara Dean. You know the Foreign Minister, Monsieur Van Trang?

(They smile and shake hands.)

Barbara. Colonel Fiedler.

BARBARA: How do you do?

(They also shake hands.)

JUDD: The Colonel's just back this evening from Binh Dinh.

BARBARA: Oh really? How are things going up there?

JUDD: I think you'll find him a very good partner.

BARBARA: Well, I hope so.

(The COLONEL *smiles.)*
COLONEL: Are they really for us yet?

8. INT. CERCLE SPORTIF. NIGHT
An annexe of the main lounge. Darker. Green baize tables have been set out for cards. BARBARA, *the* COLONEL, JUDD *and* VAN TRANG *sitting as three servants lay out their drinks and unwrap fresh packs of cards for them.*
JUDD: The Foreign Minister plays an orthodox Acol.
   (BARBARA *smiles at the* COLONEL.)
BARBARA: I play a forcing two clubs.
COLONEL: No doubt we'll get the hang of each other.
JUDD: Good. Let's cut for the deal.
   (A polite cut is silently made. The COLONEL *starts to deal, as the* MINISTER *makes formal conversation.)*
VAN TRANG: I have not been in England for too long a time.
BARBARA: No, well, I haven't been back.
VAN TRANG: Both my daughters are at Cheltenham Ladies' College.
BARBARA: Ah, well, I'm told it's a very good school.
   (She smiles and looks away to the main lounge. There a couple of bar girls have appeared, conspicuous in the otherwise discreet surroundings. They wear short slit skirts and heavy make-up. Everyone else ignores them.)
VAN TRANG: I wish I got more chance to visit them. I am told Sports Day is the highlight of the year.
   (JUDD *smiles, having picked up on the direction of* BARBARA's *look.)*
JUDD: We seem to have visitors from Mimi's Flamboyant . . .
COLONEL: Well I guess they have nowhere to go. You think there'd be somewhere . . .
   (The MINISTER *looks up for the* WAITER *who appears at once beside him.)*
VAN TRANG: *(In Vietnamese)* The women.
WAITER: *(In Vietnamese)* I'll see to it, sir.
   (The MINISTER *turns back. Looks at his cards.)*

91

VAN TRANG: It's a shortage of Americans. With so few GIs left the living is hard. What can they do? You created the industry. Now they're fed up because you're no longer here.
(The COLONEL *tries to make light of it.)*
COLONEL: Well I don't know. There are one or two of us . . .
JUDD: Some of us have friends who keep them in work.
(JUDD *smiles. The* MINISTER *ignores this. The women are led amicably away by waiters.* BARBARA *still watching.)*
VAN TRANG: One diamond.
COLONEL: A spade.
JUDD: Two hearts.
(A pause. BARBARA *is still staring at the women.)*
Barbara?
(She turns back and, without referring to her cards, shakes her head at the COLONEL.)
BARBARA: I'm sorry, partner. I'm no help at all.

9. INT. CERCLE SPORTIF. NIGHT
Later. The game is over. The four of them stroll steadily through the now deserted lounge. Behind them you can see their table being cleared. The COLONEL *and* VAN TRANG *are in front, talking quietly together.*
VAN TRANG: Will you be giving us a military briefing?
COLONEL: Certainly. There'll be a situation report. Of course, within the terms of the Paris agreement we can no longer give you military advice.
(They stroll on. VAN TRANG *makes no reaction.)*
VAN TRANG: But you have an idea?
COLONEL: I see formations. We think the North will make an offensive in the New Year. It's come to be regular . . . like the baseball season.
(There is a pause. Then casually) We'd certainly like to get to see your President Thieu.
(He steals a quick glance at VAN TRANG *who does not react.)*
As for the scale of the offensive and where it might come

from, it's a little early to say. There are certainly signs of a build-up. Maybe you should look to Tay Ninh.

(There is a slight pause. The MINISTER *looks at him. Then turns to the others.)*

VAN TRANG: Thank you, Miss Dean. An excellent evening. Colonel.

COLONEL: Minister.

JUDD: Good night.

VAN TRANG: Good night.

(He goes. They are by the main entrance. JUDD *turns casually to* BARBARA.)

JUDD: Barbara, I'll see you home in my car.

BARBARA: I arranged for a cab.

10. EXT. CERCLE SPORTIF. NIGHT

JUDD *and* BARBARA *stand for a moment outside the main entrance to the club. At once there is a giggling noise from the bushes, brief, sharp in the darkness.*

BARBARA: They're still out there.

JUDD: Who?

(She reaches into her bag for a handful of notes.)

BARBARA: Will you just take some money across?

(Before he can answer she anticipates his objections.)

Would you do it please? As a favour?

JUDD: You know it's not . . .

BARBARA: No. As a favour, Frank?

*(*JUDD *takes the money reluctantly and goes down the steps.* BARBARA *watches as he crosses the darkened drive and disappears into the bushes. She stands alone in the lit doorway of the Cercle.* JUDD *has now disappeared. Distant voices.)*

WOMAN: Thank you, Number One. You wanna fuck me?

JUDD: No. It's all right. It's a gift.

(Behind BARBARA, BOB CHESNEAU *has silently appeared. He is about 28, very intelligent, in beige cotton trousers and a short-sleeved shirt. His speech is always gentle and gracious,*

93

like a polite boy. He stands behind BARBARA, *looking out also.)*

CHESNEAU: Hi.

(She turns.)

BARBARA: Hello.

CHESNEAU: You waiting for a taxi?

(BARBARA *smiles in reply.)*

I guess the wheels have finally fallen off.

(They both smile.)

If you like I could easily help you. I have a car waiting over there.

(JUDD *has returned, his arm outstretched to* CHESNEAU. *He is bustling with confidence from a mission accomplished.)*

JUDD: Hey, Bob.

CHESNEAU: Frank, how are you?

JUDD: Do you know Barbara?

CHESNEAU: No. No, I don't.

(BARBARA *turns and smiles warmly at* JUDD.)

BARBARA: Bob's kindly offered . . . he's going to run me home.

11. INT. CAR. NIGHT

The car. They are side by side in silence. The half-lit streets of Saigon going by. CHESNEAU *driving.*

BARBARA: Where do you work?

CHESNEAU: I work at the Embassy. I'm a minor official. One of many, I'm afraid.

BARBARA: Why do you drive a Ford Pinto?

(He smiles.)

CHESNEAU: Oh I see . . .

BARBARA: I don't understand . . .

CHESNEAU: Neither do we . . .

BARBARA: The allocation. If the CIA is meant to be so secret, why do you all get issued with the same make of car?

CHESNEAU: Beats me. Perhaps a kind of arrogance. And anyway, let's face it, everyone knows. If all the cultural attachés

in Saigon were genuine, this would be the most cultured
nation on earth.
(A pause.)
I'm a spook.
(BARBARA *smiles. She looks out to the streets where the young
girls are selling flowers. They hold them out to the cars as they
go by.)*
BARBARA: Look . . .
CHESNEAU: Yeah.
BARBARA: They're still out with the jasmine. It's such a beauti-
ful town.
CHESNEAU: Yes it is. I suppose I'd forgotten.
BARBARA: Well, I know. People do.
(She looks at him. Then away.)
CHESNEAU: Where do you come from?
BARBARA: Bournemouth. You wouldn't know it. It's the English
version of Vung Tau.
CHESNEAU: By the ocean?
BARBARA: Exactly. It's where you go when you're planning to
die.
CHESNEAU: Oh yeah? Ours is called Florida.
BARBARA: Yes. Yours has the sun.

12. EXT. APARTMENT BLOCK. NIGHT
*The low white apartment block, fronted with palm trees. Ches-
neau's car stops silently in the deserted street. He gets out of the
car to go round and open the car door for her. She gets out.
There is a moment's pause, then casually:*
BARBARA: Yes. Come up.
(She goes on ahead.)

13. INT. APARTMENT. NIGHT
CHESNEAU *sitting forward on a hard chair with a glass beer in
his hands. He is in the middle of the room. His face is lit by a
single warm lamp.* BARBARA *sits on the sofa, her legs tucked
under her.*

95

CHESNEAU: It's the ultimate irony really. I joined the CIA to avoid Vietnam. Quite a few of us did the same thing. It was my law professor, he said if you want to avoid a war, the safest place to be is inside the bureaucracy. Tuck yourself away. Join the CIA.

(A pause.)

And that was it. They put me in Washington. Strategic analysis, balance of power. I was having a good time. In the way you do. I kept telling myself, well, I don't really work here, I was just avoiding the draft. Till a colleague in the department, as a joke, filled in my name. Like when you order someone *Reader's Digest*, he thought it would be funny if I were sent to Vietnam.

(He looks across at her.)

BARBARA: Would you like another beer?

CHESNEAU: Yes, I'll have one more.

(He watches as she gets up and goes to the big old fridge in the kitchen.)

You know, I can get you Heineken from the PX.

BARBARA: No really . . .

CHESNEAU: This stuff has probably killed people.

(She returns with a couple of bottles.)

BARBARA: I like '33'.

CHESNEAU: You must be tough.

(She smiles, the old hand. Then settles on the sofa, having given him one.)

BARBARA: What is your view . . . you must tell me . . . will the South be able to hold on?

CHESNEAU: That is my job. To judge that. That is precisely what I'm doing here.

(A pause. Then he gets up, putting his beer suddenly to one side.)

Thank you for the beer. I've enjoyed talking to you.

(She doesn't move, staring up at him.)

The days go by. Well, I must thank you.

(They look at each other a moment. Then he looks at the floor.)
I hope I'll see you again.

14. INT. APARTMENT. NIGHT

The room seen from the bedroom. BARBARA *sits alone at her desk in her dressing-gown.*

BARBARA: *(VO)* Dear Mum, I'm sorry it's so long since I've written. To be honest, I've been too busy at work. You'll be pleased with my cheque. A little bit extra. The bank have just come through with my raise.

(In close-up her hand as she slips the cheque into the already finished letter.)

(VO) Life here continues very much as usual.

(Her face, for the first time in close-up, as she licks the envelope.)

(VO) The Year of the Tiger will soon be the Year of the Cat.

15. INT. BANK. DAY

HENDERSON *standing at one of the metal grilles opposite a shock-haired young Vietnamese,* PHU, *of about 25. He is very angry.*

HENDERSON: I'm sorry. I have to refuse you. It's simply impossible to take all that money out.

(He looks sideways at QUOC *who is at a nearby till.* BARBARA *looks up from her desk.)*

There are government regulations which expressly forbid the export of large sums.

16. INT. HALIWELL'S OFFICE. DAY

BARBARA *appearing at the door of Haliwell's office.* HALIWELL *is writing at his desk.*

BARBARA: Mr Haliwell . . . I wonder . . . I think Mr Henderson may be needing some assistance out there.

*(*QUOC's *face appears in the doorway behind her, still, serious. But* HALIWELL *carries on writing.)*

97

HALIWELL: Right. In a moment.
BARBARA: Could you come quickly?
HALIWELL: Yes.
(He carries on writing. He does not look up. Quietly, into his work, without moving) I'm on my way.

17. INT. BANK. DAY
HALIWELL, QUOC *and* BARBARA *moving together like a group of floor-walkers, fast, from a great distance towards the incident.* PHU *takes a small revolver from his pocket.* HENDERSON *is standing opposite.*
PHU: I have a gun.
HENDERSON: Yes.
PHU: I demand my money.
HENDERSON: If you'd like to talk to the manager . . .
(HALIWELL *steps forward from the group to stand beside* HENDERSON.)
HALIWELL: Mr . . .
HENDERSON: Phu.
HALIWELL: Mr Phu, perhaps I can help you.
PHU: I want my money.
HALIWELL: Yes. Yes, of course.
(He begins to move across to the grille door between the back and front of the bank.)
If you'd like to come into my office. . . .
(He swings the door open and stands directly opposite PHU *who is holding the gun.* HALIWELL *looks him straight in the eye.)*
Perhaps I might relieve you of that gun.

18. INT. BANK. DAY
The bank closed. Afternoon. HENDERSON *is laughing, sitting on the edge of Barbara's desk. Way behind him the tellers are locking up their drawers.*
HENDERSON: Well, I must say, you have to hand it to him. Haliwell really came through.

98

BARBARA: He was lucky.

HENDERSON: It was a tactic. I think we should all be grateful it worked.

(He laughs again. QUOC *comes and sits down near them, quietly resuming his work.)*

To be honest, I was seriously frightened. *(His tone is suddenly intimate.)* You were bloody great.

BARBARA: It worked out well.

(HENDERSON *smiles a moment, vacantly.)*

HENDERSON: All right, Quoc?

QUOC: Yes thank you, Mr Henderson.

(Behind him, a girl who looks to be no more than 14 is getting down from a high stool, picking up her bag, and walking out of frame.)

One of the tellers has decided to leave.

19. INT. APARTMENT. NIGHT

BARBARA *sitting reading a book. Her legs characteristically tucked up under her. Like a quiet animal. She turns a page, silently. Then looks up.* CHESNEAU *has appeared at the open door to the living room. He carries his jacket and his shirt is marked with sweat.*

CHESNEAU: You should lock the door. I think you're crazy. Do you have any idea of how dangerous it is?

BARBARA: Nobody wants a white English woman.

(She smiles. She doesn't move from the sofa.)

How are you?

(A pause. Then he moves into the room, casually putting a small bunch of flowers down on the table, carelessly, on its side.)

CHESNEAU: You've not been at the club.

BARBARA: Have you been looking?

(He nods.)

No. I've been reading my books. It's wonderful here in the evenings. The silence, lately. The peace.

(He turns at the window and looks at her.)

99

CHESNEAU: I am very emotionally stupid. This is . . . this has always been true. I never know. Even when it's incredibly blatant.

BARBARA: I think this time you probably have the idea.

(He nods slightly.)

CHESNEAU: Yeah, I thought I did.

BARBARA: Yes. You have it.

CHESNEAU: Ah. I came round to check.

BARBARA: What a relief . . .

CHESNEAU: Yeah . . .

BARBARA: The embarrassment. If it turned out that you'd got it wrong.

CHESNEAU: Yeah, well, I'd thought of that. . . .

(He stands, nodding again.)

It was a factor. Will you have a cigarette?

BARBARA: No. No thanks.

(He stands a moment, holding the pack out.)

CHESNEAU: Hey, I was right. Terrific. CIA! Intelligence, huh?

20. INT. APARTMENT. NIGHT

The bed seen from the living room. They are lying together, still. He has his back against the pillows, she is stretched out across him. Her face is on his chest. A single sheet covers the rest of them. We move in as they talk very quietly.

BARBARA: And are you there?

CHESNEAU: No, it's done without me.

BARBARA: What, they're . . .

CHESNEAU: They're beaten, then put back in their cells. Today I went crazy, my best prisoner had been beaten to hell. His shirt fell open, he had scars . . . welts, right across here . . .

(He gestures across his own chest.)

BARBARA: It's wrong.

CHESNEAU: Yeah. But it's also just stupid. He's an important enemy source.

(There is a pause.)

For ten days I've been sitting there. Patiently. A small

100

wooden table. Just leading him on. I get in today, someone's
got restless, no point in waiting for Chesneau any more. . . .
It's stupid. The agents you capture, they're your life-blood.
You don't go and hit them in the mouth. Hit people in the
mouth, they just go stubborn, or they just tell you what you
most want to hear.

(He shakes his head.)

Get the facts first, get things sorted, be sure you've really got
hold of the facts. Then later . . . hell, throw him out of a
helicopter. But afterwards.

BARBARA: Does that happen?

(He turns and looks at her.)

CHESNEAU: *(Quietly)* Of course.

21. INT. BATHROOM. NIGHT

Later. BARBARA *is sitting on a small wooden stool, her back
against the wall, with her feet out in front of her on a chair. She
is in her dressing-gown.* CHESNEAU's *face is below her; he is
stretched out in the bath smoking a Marlboro. The only other
sound is the occasional ripple of the water.*

BARBARA: The men at the bank, oh, they're quite easygoing.
We've all been here for so long. The Scots are always bankers.
Or else engineers. *(She smiles.)* The funniest is . . . do you
know the British Council?

CHESNEAU: No.

BARBARA: You don't know, but they still have a library here. To
encourage the spread of English culture. Good idea, yes?
Here in Saigon?

(They smile.)

I went there. There's now just one girl running it. She's Vietnamese. She sits at a desk. I went up to her. She doesn't speak
English.

(They look at each other. They laugh.)

CHESNEAU: Oh yes. Well, sure.

22. INT. APARTMENT. DAWN
Light beginning to hit the blinds. BARBARA *sitting on the sofa, with* CHESNEAU's *head on her lap, curled up like a child pressed against her breasts. The room held.*

23. INT. BANK. DAY
Morning. BARBARA *in close-up standing waiting at Haliwell's office door as* HALIWELL *arrives for work. A well-defined routine. She is smiling slightly as he goes past her.*
HALIWELL: Good morning, Barbara. How are you?
BARBARA: Fine, Mr Haliwell. Thanks.
   (She starts to unload the pile of ledgers from her arms. He picks up The Times *from his side of the desk and casually throws it to her.)*
HALIWELL: Look at this. Strikes. Industrial chaos. The whole country seems to be going to hell.
   (She unfolds it with one hand, less than curious.)
BARBARA: Good Lord.
HALIWELL: I mean, it's national insanity. The unions seem to want to run the whole show. I must say, though, one can count one's blessings.
   (He is hanging up his coat and now turns, smiling.)
We can all be grateful we're living out here.

24. EXT. OCKHAM'S HOUSE. DAY
The lawn behind Ockham's detached clapboard house. The whole scene gleaming in the sun. There is a party for about fifty people, a mixture of races, all casually dressed. Children are jumping into the portable pool which is next to the house. At the centre a tall, intense man in his early fifties, with sunglasses. He is wearing a shirt and slacks, greeting guests as they arrive. He is JACK OCKHAM.
OCKHAM: Hi . . . how are you? Nice to see you.
   (CHESNEAU *appears,* BARBARA *a pace behind.)*
Bob, how are you?
CHESNEAU: This is Barbara Dean. Jack Ockham.

(OCKHAM *smiles slightly and takes her hand.*)

OCKHAM: I'm very glad you could make it.

CHESNEAU: Barbara works in the bank.

OCKHAM: Good.

(*He nods slightly.* CHESNEAU *unsure of how to introduce her.*) Well, Merry Christmas.

BARBARA: Thank you. And Merry Christmas to you.

(*Behind them servants are carrying three huge steaming-hot turkeys to the white tables which are laid out on the lawn.* OCKHAM *passes on to greet the next guests, a short Vietnamese* GENERAL *and his taller* WIFE. *They are heard in the background as we follow* BARBARA *and* CHESNEAU, *walking into the mass of the party.*)

Are we a couple?

CHESNEAU: What?

BARBARA: In public?

CHESNEAU: I don't know. Do you know?

BARBARA: No.

(*They both smile.*)

I enjoy the uncertainty.

CHESNEAU: Yes. Let's not be. For the moment let's stay good friends.

25. EXT. LAWN. DAY

Later. A burst of noise and laughter from a table just behind our group who are CHESNEAU, BARBARA, FIEDLER, JUDD *and* OCKHAM *who sits slightly apart.* FIEDLER *has a paper hat. There are streamers and the debris of a good meal. The atmosphere is easy and slightly drunk.*

OCKHAM: Bob's never understood the aid allocation. You've never understood it.

CHESNEAU: No, well, that's true.

(COLONEL FIEDLER *explains, for* BARBARA*'s benefit.*)

FIEDLER: We want Congress to vote three hundred million dollars to prove they support Thieu's regime.

OCKHAM: Yeah.

103

FIEDLER: Now in fact . . . three hundred million, well it's not nearly enough, with the economy as bad as it is. We need more than that. But at least it would be symbolic—a symbol of the American intention to help.

(BARBARA *looks across at* CHESNEAU. *He looks down at his hands.*)

Now back home there's a lot of opposition . . .

OCKHAM: Left-wing elements . . .

FIEDLER: Liberals, yeah. People who never liked the war in the first place, who are now saying we should just get out, go home, forget about it. Abandon our friends.

(He shrugs slightly, as if suppressing the strong feeling he has.)

Well, I don't think that's a viable option. I don't think that's what Americans should do.

(BARBARA *frowns slightly.*)

BARBARA: But isn't the problem . . .

(She pauses.)

CHESNEAU: What?

BARBARA: No, I shouldn't say.

(There is a pause. FIEDLER *is looking at* CHESNEAU.)

CHESNEAU: Go on.

BARBARA: No, I really . . . I don't know much about it.

(She smiles and looks away.)

OCKHAM: *(With characteristic quiet)* Barbara, you must say what you think.

(She turns and looks at them.)

BARBARA: I would have thought the problem you have here is the money will go to a particular regime. A regime whose reputation is for corruption. And there are political prisoners as well . . .

(FIEDLER *easy at the familiarity of this charge.*)

FIEDLER: Oh well, sure, but . . .

BARBARA: Please, I'm not saying . . . for all I know Thieu is the best man. It's just that if he goes . . . you will go with

him. You may be sitting on a branch that's withered. That's
all.

(A pause. CHESNEAU *is looking at her.)*

FIEDLER: Well, I don't think . . .

BARBARA: It's . . .

FIEDLER: There's no sign of that. The regime is hardly threatened from within.

BARBARA: No?

(He is staring at her, frowning.)

FIEDLER: Barbara, there's only one enemy. That's the enemy
that's waiting out there.

26. EXT. LAWN. NIGHT

*At once, the whole scene seen from the bushes, far away and at
night. There is now a barbecue around which people are gathered and others are jumping into the darkened pool. Raised
voices and laughter. It is eerie. The shot held.*

27. EXT. HOUSE. NIGHT

BARBARA *and* CHESNEAU *left sitting alone on the now deserted
lawn, as the party continues indoors. Distant whooping around
a lit tree indoors.*

CHESNEAU: I decided . . . while you were talking, watching
you arguing it out . . . I thought tomorrow I'm going to go in
there. It's time I told everyone what I really think.

(BARBARA is watching him closely.)

We're so obsessed with this aid allocation that we pretend that
things are much worse than they are. We think that only by
exaggerating are we going to get all the money we need. *(He
shakes his head.)* All the time we're saying, it's coming, it's
coming, quick, give us money, give us aid. But that battle
back there in Washington has become more real to us than
anything here.

*(There is a particularly loud whoop from the house, as of a
violent party game.)*

105

BARBARA: I must say, from the way they're behaving . . . it doesn't look as if they really think it's the end.

CHESNEAU: No, of course not. Charades.

(He pauses, then moves his glass away.)

But meanwhile the facts get pushed out the way.

28. INT. APARTMENT. NIGHT

The apartment still at night. BARBARA *in bed. The sound of a very distant explosion, a rumble in the night.* CHESNEAU *is seen to be standing at the window, with a towel wrapped round his middle.*

BARBARA: What is it?

CHESNEAU: Oh it's the gas dump. It's always the gas dump when it's that close.

(He holds the blind apart, staring out absently.)

They pretend. They send up rockets. But really the job is done from the inside.

BARBARA: What d'you mean?

CHESNEAU: Well, they always put up the firecrackers. . . .

(He smiles and makes an arc with his arm.)

Great lights in the night. So you think it's being bombed. But in fact there's always an employee working for the VC on the inside, all he's done is slip a detonator in.

(He turns and looks at her. The noise has died.)

All the rest is show. They like to do it. I don't know why.

BARBARA: Perhaps because subversion's too easy.

(He looks across at her.)

CHESNEAU: Something like that.

29. INT. APARTMENT. NIGHT

BARBARA *in her white dressing-gown sitting directly across from* CHESNEAU *at a small table. He is still in his towel. They are sipping tea from small Chinese cups, in the middle of the night.*

CHESNEAU: Can you give me an idea of England?

BARBARA: Well. . . . *(She smiles.)* The place is very wet.

106

Which makes its greenness almost iridescent. It is almost indecently green.
(They smile.)
The people are—odd. They're cruel to each other. Mostly in silent . . . in unexpected ways. It's an emotional cruelty. You feel watched, disapproved of all the time.
CHESNEAU: That's why you got away?
BARBARA: There's a terrible pressure, all these little hedgerows squeezing you in, tight little lines of upright houses. Everyone spying on everyone else.
(She looks over at him and smiles.)
I'm not even . . . an unconventional woman. I need only that amount of air. But I can't get it in England.
(There is a pause. CHESNEAU is looking at her.)
I know what you're thinking. Will I ever go back?

30. INT. BANK. DAY
The hustle of the bank at lunchtime. Shafts of sunlight falling as in a cathedral across the back area, while at the front it is very busy before lunch. BARBARA is at her desk, staring hopelessly at a sheaf of papers. QUOC comes over to wait for her verdict.
BARBARA: Quoc, I'm afraid this isn't possible. Really there's no question of this.
(She looks up at him regretfully.)
It's pointless investing money in transport now the Vietcong are blowing up roads.
QUOC: Shall I say this to him?
BARBARA: Yes. If you want to. I mean . . . yes. It's impossible. How can I possibly defend an investment when we're approaching the worst time of year? I mean of course, yes, when the rains come, I'll consider it again. But until the rains . . . there is uncertainty. Can you tell him?
QUOC: Yes. As you say.
(HENDERSON has appeared at the desk, hovering. His shirt is

cleaner, his beard trimmer than ever. QUOC *is putting more papers on Barbara's desk.)*
That. Just a signature.
BARBARA: Hello, Donald.
HENDERSON: I wonder, could I have a word?
BARBARA: Yes of course. What can I do for you?
QUOC: *(Discreetly)* And another signature there.
(HENDERSON *waits for* QUOC *to finish.* BARBARA *speaks meanwhile.)*
BARBARA: Tell Mr Haliwell about these decisions. If you want my judgement checked against his . . .
QUOC: No, it isn't necessary.
(He takes the papers and goes. BARBARA *sighs.)*
BARBARA: Oh Lord, do you think it's a personal friend?
(HENDERSON *shrugs slightly.)*
HENDERSON: My point is this. I need to ask you. . . .
(He pauses, uncomfortable.)
Do you think I'll ever be promoted in here?
BARBARA: What are you saying?
(She looks at him, levelly.)
You mean you're leaving?
HENDERSON: Yes, well, possibly. I'm not really sure.
(He looks down, embarrassed.)
I mean, there's you and above you there's Haliwell. Neither of you seem as if you're likely to retire. So the fact is . . . I got round to thinking . . . well, I've been offered a job in Hong Kong.
BARBARA: Good. You must take it.
HENDERSON: Yes. I would like to. That's right.
(They stare at each other.)
BARBARA: Well, that's nice. We'll arrange a party.
(He looks at her, then suddenly bursts, like an overflowing sink.)
HENDERSON: You know, I am most terribly in love.
(She looks panic-stricken round the bank.)
BARBARA: Yes, well, I think this is . . .

108

HENDERSON: Honestly.

BARBARA: Hardly the moment . . .

HENDERSON: Just the thought I might not see you again . . .

(BARBARA *turns relieved to* QUOC *who has returned with more papers.*)

BARBARA: Yes?

(HENDERSON *suddenly shouts at the top of his voice.*)

HENDERSON: Oh God, Quoc, will you never ever leave us? Can't we have one moment on our own?

(There is a pause. All over the bank people stop work and look up. QUOC *is shocked, but looks impassively at* HENDERSON.)

QUOC: I'm sorry.

BARBARA: No . . . You must stay here. Mr Henderson is just a little upset.

(She looks up at HENDERSON, *quietly furious.)*

HENDERSON: Yes. God, I'm sorry.

BARBARA: He doesn't mean it. He had no intention of being so rude.

(HENDERSON *shakes his head weakly.*)

HENDERSON: Really I'm sorry, it's unforgivable . . .

(QUOC *looks at them, nods.*)

QUOC: In a few moments, I shall return.

31. INT. BANK. EVENING

The bank, dark now. Among the empty desks HENDERSON *sits with his head in his hands.* BARBARA *is leaning against a desk nearby. Beyond them in the distance a young Vietnamese girl with a long pole closes the shutters on the high windows.*

HENDERSON: Oh my God, Barbara, I can tell you despise me.

BARBARA: Have I said anything?

HENDERSON: No. Not at all. It's just . . . your general demeanour. You behave as if I'm doing something wrong.

(BARBARA *looks down at him, as if a little surprised.*)

I do have to tell you, I've been going crazy . . .

BARBARA: Well, in that case it's best that you leave. Hong Kong is a good place to forget me. *(She smiles slightly, amused at*

109

the ludicrousness of the remark.) So you'll be much happier there.
(She is looking at the floor.)
HENDERSON: I would like . . . I feel you disapprove of me.
(She does not answer.)
You feel I'm cowardly, that's right? (BARBARA *smiles, this time bitterly, at the inadequacy of what she will say.)*
BARBARA: I think that we . . . who were not born here . . . should make sure we go with dignity.
(There is a pause.)
That's all.

32. INT. BANK. DAY
Morning. The bank is busy again. Tellers moving back and forth. In the middle of the back area, HENDERSON, *turned away from us, is clearing out his desk, like an expelled pupil, as the commerce of the bank goes on.*
BARBARA: *(VO)* Donald *did* leave with comparative dignity.
(BARBARA *watches him, from behind her desk.)*
Compared with some of the rest of us, I mean.
(She turns. Her eye catches camera.)

PART TWO

33. INT. CAR. DAY
Fade-up inside the car. CHESNEAU's *face as he drives through early-morning Saigon. There is a cigarette hanging from his mouth. The cool morning goes by outside. The image holds. Then after a few seconds . . .*
BARBARA: *(VO)* I used to see Bob whenever it was possible. When we could we met, discreetly, in my room. As time went by it became much harder . . .

34. EXT. EMBASSY. DAY
The great white bulk of the American Embassy in Saigon, cut out against the morning sky. Palm trees and lawns in front of the huge square building. The gates open, the barrier goes up, Chesneau's Pinto goes through, with a greeting from the guard.
BARBARA: *(VO)* He could only manage an occasional hour. Anyone who worked in that great white building seemed to vanish inside for the day . . .

35. INT. EMBASSY LOBBY. DAY
CHESNEAU *crosses the guarded lobby of the Embassy, carrying a briefcase. He makes for the elevator, showing his pass as he goes.*
BARBARA: *(VO)* It was a city inside a city. Always, it seemed, with a life of its own.
(The elevator doors close.)

36. INT. CORRIDOR. DAY
CHESNEAU *walks along the long neon-lit corridor at the spine of CIA headquarters on the fifth floor of the Embassy. A jump in*

111

sound: typewriters, telexes, shredders, people calling from room to room.

BARBARA: *(VO)* On the fifth floor of the Embassy, the New Year had begun much as they'd expected. Offensives from the North had started on time . . .

(Lines of doors on either side, through which we see desk workers, strategic analysts. The maps, the desks, the charts, the projections, the files. Piles and piles of paperwork. Everyone is in civilian clothing.)

(VO) The town of Phuoc Binh fell at the beginning of January.

(A cry of 'Hi, Bob' from one of the doors.)

(VO) But then Ban me Thuot followed early in March.

37. INT. OFFICE. DAY

CHESNEAU *standing with his secretary* LINDA *in the communal secretaries' office. She is 24, blonde, big-jawed and plaid-skirted, in the Mid-Western way. He is nodding at some papers she is showing him.*

BARBARA: *(VO)* Somehow up till then nothing really told them this was going to be the long-awaited end . . .

(CHESNEAU nods as the SECRETARY explains a document to him.)

(VO) They'd lived through so many of these annual readjustments, at first they'd just assumed it was another of the same. . . .

38. INT. CORRIDOR. DAY

CHESNEAU *walking on, purposefully, down the corridor towards the far end.*

BARBARA: *(VO)* Of course, I suppose if they'd just looked around them, if they'd ever just stopped and thought . . .

(CHESNEAU reaches the end room. The door is open. Ockham's office. There are ten people sitting round in the deep-blue carpeted office, with a pine desk where OCKHAM is. CHESNEAU stops at the open door.)

(VO) But somehow . . . all of us . . . our eye was else-where.

(OCKHAM looks up from behind his desk.)

(VO) When we realized, it was too late.

39. INT. OFFICE. DAY

At once we join the scene which has plainly already been long in progress. A young OFFICER lectures from a wall map of Vietnam, pointing with a short stick. Sitting round in the other chairs we see COLONEL FIEDLER and JUDD, among a mixture of analysts and military. OCKHAM is standing staring ahead, a picture of President Ford behind him. CHESNEAU sits down, as we pick up the OFFICER in mid-brief.

OFFICER: . . . hemmed in on the road. The South has lost fif-teen hamlets in twenty-four hours. Here. On the road be-tween Quang Tri and Hue. *(He points further down the map.)* Two district towns gone here in Quang Tin. The North head-ing down towards Tam Ky. *(Further down.)* Ban me Thuot here, of course, consolidated. And the anticipated push to Tay Ninh. . . . *(He points.)* Signs of that are finally happening. This morning they lost the town of Tri Tam.

(He stands a moment, almost apologetic.)

FIEDLER: Jesus Christ, they're coming out everywhere . . .

OCKHAM: No, it's not so. . . .

(He nods at the OFFICER to sit down.)

It's logical, I'm afraid. Once President Thieu decided to aban-don the Highlands, everything that's happened makes logical sense.

(There is a pause.)

FIEDLER: Do we know more?

OCKHAM: Joan . . .

(OCKHAM, anticipating, has already nodded at JOAN MACKIN-TOSH, who has got up. She is a CIA analyst, a brisk, well-built woman of about 40, in a pleated summer dress. She goes over to the map.)

MACKINTOSH: We have this from Thieu's Cabinet.

(FIEDLER *looks at* OCKHAM, *surprised.*)

OCKHAM: We now have an agent in there.

MACKINTOSH: He explains. He says there is a new strategy.
(With a cloth she wipes the old marks from the laminated map.)
I'm afraid it was only invented this week.
(She takes a Pentel and draws a thick line horizontally across South Vietnam from just above Tay Ninh to Nha Trang, so that the country is neatly divided three-quarters of the way down.)
That . . . a defensive line. . . .
(Then she draws three tiny semicircles, way up on the coast in the North, all isolated from the main defensive area. They are around Quang-Nai, Tam-Ky and Hue and Danang.)
Here . . . these enclaves . . . these coastal towns . . .
(She turns back.) Nothing else. The rest is abandoned.

FIEDLER: *(Quietly)* My God.

MACKINTOSH: *(As quietly)* There we are.
(There is a silence. As if to fill it, apologetically, in contrast to her earlier manner, MACKINTOSH *explains.)* It isn't . . . we don't think it would be a bad strategy. It's always been an option the South has had. What is disastrous is simply the speed of it. It was intended this option should cover six months. Instead of which it's been three days now since it was implemented and of course . . . *(She looks to* OCKHAM, *as if deferring to him, tying herself up slightly as she finishes.)*
. . . to do with its suddenness, I think . . . now it's happening, well, we all know . . . it does seem as if it's panic all round.
(There is a long pause. OCKHAM *stares ahead. From the back* CHESNEAU *speaks quietly.)*

CHESNEAU: Where's the Ambassador?
*(*OCKHAM *doesn't answer at once.)*
Still getting his teeth fixed?

OCKHAM: I have it here.

114

(He nods and reaches among the pile of telexes on his desk. He reads from the appropriate wire.)

Minor orthodontal surgery was completed in North Carolina last week.

CHESNEAU: And is he coming back?

OCKHAM: Yeah. Eventually. *(He reads from the cable again.)* He says 'No panic.' That's it. 'The situation is not yet serious.' *(He drops it on the desk, then quietly)* I think that maybe we'd better leave it there.

(He nods to dismiss them. People rise uncertainly, CHESNEAU *looking at* JUDD. OCKHAM *at once starts to talk to* FIEDLER.)

Thank you, everyone. Colonel, if you got a moment . . .

(But we go with CHESNEAU *and* JUDD, *leaving together in a group of agents, talking under their breath.)*

CHESNEAU: It's Loonyville. Land of the Loonies!

JUDD: That's right.

40. INT. CORRIDOR. DAY

Continuous. As they come out into the corridor and are able to raise their voices, the hysteria begins to seep.

CHESNEAU: Oh my God, the spooks are going *crazy.*

(People around them scatter, still talking, as they go on down the corridor, JUDD *already tapping satirically at his teeth with his fingernail and smiling.)*

JUDD: Teeth!

CHESNEAU: Yeah.

JUDD: What's he going to do with them? Bite the fucking VC in the neck?

(They go on down the corridor. Suddenly the remains of the meeting has broken up and all the other agents and officers have disappeared, leaving JUDD *and* CHESNEAU *the last two.* CHESNEAU *puts his hand on* JUDD*'s arm as they disappear.)*

CHESNEAU: Frank. Suppose it happens. And we evacuate . . .

(They disappear. The deserted corridor. We catch CHESNEAU*'s voice from round the corner.)*

Has anyone thought to look at the plans?
(A pause. We look at the empty corridor.)

41. EXT. WASTEGROUND. NIGHT
Chesneau's Pinto silently drawing up on a piece of wrecked Saigon suburb. It is so quiet it is as if he has turned the engine off. He comes to a halt. There is just open ground, with some shacks away in the distance, and alone in the wasteground a small tin garage. CHESNEAU *lights a cigarette. He sits a moment in the car. Then he gets out and begins to walk across the silent wasteground.*

42. INT. GARAGE. NIGHT
CHESNEAU *opening the corrugated-iron door. The night seen briefly behind him as he slips in. The door closes. At the end a man is sitting on a crate, behind some tyres. He is 40, thin, with exceptionally bad skin. He wears sun-glasses. His name is* NHIEU. CHESNEAU *speaks quietly.*
CHESNEAU: Hi. How are you?
NHIEU: I am well, thank you.
CHESNEAU: That's good.
NHIEU: I want this to be our final meeting. I don't want money. I want documents out.
(CHESNEAU stands still at the door.)
CHESNEAU: Well, if you like. It may not be necessary. I don't think anyone knows what you do.
NHIEU: It is a condition.
(CHESNEAU nods slightly, in assent.)
When?
CHESNEAU: Your papers? Soon.
NHIEU: Tomorrow. And travellers' cheques. American Express.
(NHIEU's voice is firm. There is a slight pause.)
CHESNEAU: Please tell me first what you have from Hanoi.
NHIEU: There was a Cabinet meeting last night. It is now the intention of the Government of the North to press the war as far as it will go.

116

CHESNEAU: Yes, but is it. . . ?

NHIEU: It will be military.

CHESNEAU: What makes you say that?

NHIEU: They call it blood scent. *(He gestures to his nose.)* The smell of blood in their noses. They will fight, all the way to Saigon.

(CHESNEAU *is seen to weigh this up, then decide to go on.)*

CHESNEAU: You see, the thought was they might stop short of the city . . .

(NHIEU *shakes his head at once.)*

NHIEU: No.

CHESNEAU: And negotiate for a coalition from strength.

NHIEU: Up till last night, yes, there was a faction. But they are defeated. They will fight their way in.

(CHESNEAU *looks at him, then goes on.)*

CHESNEAU: This time, I'm sorry, I will have to ask you how close the source is.

NHIEU: Has he ever been wrong?

(NHIEU *looks straight at him, holding his stare.)*

CHESNEAU: When?

NHIEU: Three weeks. The end of April. *(He smiles slightly.)* I am not staying. I will be gone.

43. EXT. WASTEGROUND. NIGHT
The two men pacing together slowly back across the ground. They look small against the vastness of the night, and the tone is of two elder statesmen.

NHIEU: I have a cousin in Omaha, Nebraska.

CHESNEAU: Ah.

NHIEU: He has a business selling paint.

CHESNEAU: Ah yes. *(He steals a quick glance at him.)* It's very quiet in Nebraska.

NHIEU: You are saying I will find no business as a pimp?

(CHESNEAU *shrugs slightly.)*

CHESNEAU: Well, I don't know. It's a land of opportunity.

NHIEU: I was hoping also, I might take some girls?

117

(They stop, CHESNEAU *registering the request, but not react-ing. They have reached the car.)*
CHESNEAU: I will try.
(He is about to get in.)
Thank you. You've been a great help to us.
NHIEU: The documents.
CHESNEAU: Yes. I will see it's arranged.

44. INT. OFFICES. NIGHT

The deserted CIA offices at dead of night. The secretaries' shared office is completely quiet, and through the open door we see CHESNEAU *at work by a single lamp.*
He reaches for a clean yellow legal pad, and quickly writes a few Vietnamese names on it. Then he pulls open a drawer in the side of his desk and takes out a fat, black address book. He opens it. It is thick, bulging, messy. Years of writing in both English and Vietnamese. He flicks a couple of times over some pages, then starts systematically transferring names from the book to his pad. Crossfade to:

45. INT. OFFICE. DAWN

CHESNEAU *sitting back at his desk, the work complete in front of him, the morning light coming through the blinds. There's a pause. Then he gets up and picks up the list, walks off down the corridor.*

46. INT. OCKHAM'S OFFICE. DAY

OCKHAM *is already at his desk, in shirt-sleeves. He has a cup of coffee at his side, and he is sitting reading the day's telexes with his legs up on the table.* CHESNEAU *comes in quietly at the door.*
CHESNEAU: Jack, you're in. *(He nods at a few sheets of paper he has left on the desk top.)* I left that for you.
OCKHAM: Yeah, I got it.
CHESNEAU: Did you take a look?
(OCKHAM nods slightly.)
I've been making a list. *(He approaches the desk with his*

118

yellow legal pad.) Here's a list of our two hundred most important local contacts. They should be the first we take out. *(He settles down to explain.)* I think the way we do it is, each department draws up a list of its most sensitive men . . .

OCKHAM: Bob, I don't disagree with you. But the Ambassador has to say when. *(He goes on before* CHESNEAU *can interrupt.)* I've already called him. He arrived back in the country last night. (CHESNEAU *is looking at him, mistrustfully.)*

CHESNEAU: Jack, these are the people who've actively worked for us . . .

OCKHAM: Sure.

CHESNEAU: There's a whole dependent community here. Don't say if the Communists finally get here, we're just going to leave them to be murdered in their beds.

OCKHAM: No question of that. We take them with us. *(He pauses, as calm as ever.)* The question is one of time-scale, that's all.

CHESNEAU: Well, in three weeks . . .

OCKHAM: You don't have to argue. At least you don't have to argue with me.

(He smiles slightly, and looks across at CHESNEAU.)*

The Ambassador's read the report of your agent. He's insisting he sees you himself.

47. INT. AMBASSADOR'S OFFICE. DAY

The Ambassador's office is lined in dark wood. It has a deep-green carpet and fine desk, with flags behind it and photographs of the Ambassador with successive Presidents—Johnson, Nixon, Ford. The AMBASSADOR *is a very tall man in his early sixties in a tropical suit. He is sandy-haired, with a disconcerting habit of sometimes seeming neither to see you nor hear you. He gets up as soon as* CHESNEAU *and* OCKHAM *come into the room, making low murmurs as he settles them in chairs.*

OCKHAM: Ambassador.

AMBASSADOR: Hi. Good morning. *(He gestures towards a chair.)*

119

Why don't you sit down?
(As they settle, the AMBASSADOR *wanders, making vague noises.)*
Bob . . . OK . . . Jack, how you doing?
(Then he settles at his own desk.)
Right. Here we are then. . . . *(He looks at* CHESNEAU.) I read your report. I have to tell you . . . I don't admire it. This is not the sort of thing I like to read. This war has always been a great test of character . . . at this time more than ever perhaps. *(He now gestures at the report on the desk.)* This simply contradicts all our information. This 'blood scent' theory . . .
CHESNEAU: Yeah.
(The AMBASSADOR *stops, waiting for* CHESNEAU *to say more.)*
The agent is good.
AMBASSADOR: I'm afraid I simply don't accept that. Nothing he says squares with the picture we have. I have read it. Thank you for submitting it. But I shall not credit it when making policy.
(He smiles at OCKHAM.)
OCKHAM: I think that's right.
AMBASSADOR: I'm telling Washington the North are still keen to negotiate . . .
(The AMBASSADOR *has sat back now, and is off on his own tack.)*
This latest round of fighting has been very bracing. It's led to some decisions which were long overdue. President Thieu has succeeded in stripping down the country, he's made it a much more defensible shape. The area we're left with is much more logical, that's the benefit of strategic withdrawal. Now when we fight we're in the right positions. As soon as they see that, the Communists will stop. That's the moment we'll be able to negotiate . . .
CHESNEAU: Sir, I don't think it'll happen like that.
(There is a pause. The AMBASSADOR *smiles easily.)*
AMBASSADOR: Well, it won't happen if everyone panics . . . if everyone starts spreading depression and alarm . . .

CHESNEAU: No, it's just . . .

(He looks for support to OCKHAM, *who gives none.)*
Our reports from the military indicate a chronic problem of morale.

(The AMBASSADOR *shifts slightly in his chair.)*

AMBASSADOR: I wonder sometimes if we don't project that. I mean, if the problem isn't more in ourselves. Because we ourselves are a little bit panicky . . . *(He pauses, hanging the sentence in the air.)* So then we kind of see it in the Vietnamese.

(CHESNEAU *starts again, calmly, trying to keep to the facts.)*

CHESNEAU: Sir, I'm worried we corrupt our intelligence. All last year we said things were bad. That was to dramatize, to secure an aid allocation. Now you're asking us to say things are good.

AMBASSADOR: Yes well, God, man, I still need money . . .

CHESNEAU: What?

AMBASSADOR: That's exactly why your stuff has got to be suppressed. *(He gestures angrily at Chesneau's report.)* Congress is hardly going to vote us more money if they believe that South Vietnam's about to be destroyed.

CHESNEAU: So you're . . .

(But the AMBASSADOR *has suddenly started raising his voice.)*

AMBASSADOR: And it's *not* going to be! God, how often do I have to say? *(He suddenly starts shouting, with hurt and bewilderment.)* What is this in us? Some kind of *death wish?* Some kind of wishing the whole thing would end?

(There is a pause.)

CHESNEAU: *(As tactfully as he can)* I think our first duty is to anyone who helped us. It's our job to get those people out . . .

AMBASSADOR: Out of the question. No evacuation. I'm not doing anything that smells of defeat.

CHESNEAU: Sir, I can promise it won't be conspicuous . . .

AMBASSADOR: Oh yes, that's fine. What? Planes overhead? *(He*

121

makes an angry gesture to the sky.) Great lines at Tan Son Nhut airport? Oh my God, yes, we really need that.

(CHESNEAU interrupts before he finishes.)

CHESNEAU: No, I am saying . . . some of the Vietnamese commanders, the men who are out in the field right now, the reason they are fighting so badly is because we've made no plans for their families and friends. Now if we could get that worry removed for them . . .

(The AMBASSADOR turns to OCKHAM.)

AMBASSADOR: He's saying he would like us to prepare for defeat.

(CHESNEAU insists at once.)

CHESNEAU: No, I'm not.

AMBASSADOR: There would be chaos.

CHESNEAU: There'll be even greater chaos if we delay. If we leave it to the very last minute, can you imagine what that's going to be like?

(There is a pause. The AMBASSADOR looks at him.)

AMBASSADOR: Chesneau, my aim is exactly to avoid that. There will be no last minute here.

CHESNEAU: Sir . . .

AMBASSADOR: The North will stop short and I will negotiate. But it's essential I do that from strength.

(CHESNEAU is about to interrupt again.)

That is why I need a new aid allocation. I've asked for seven hundred million this week. The President has promised he will get it from Congress. *(He sits back.)* Until then we are going to sit tight.

CHESNEAU: *(Very quiet now)* But sir . . . with respect . . . you didn't get it last time. In effect you're gambling with thousands of lives.

AMBASSADOR: We are going to prove our absolute friendship.

CHESNEAU: Even if it costs our friends their own lives?

(There is a pause. The debate is over. The AMBASSADOR speaks, full of sorrow.)

AMBASSADOR: Bob. I don't like to see you hysterical. I know the

work has gotten very hard. I don't like to see you join the conspiracy. *(He looks up at him a moment.)* You of all people. *(His own melancholy is so apparent that* CHESNEAU *cannot reply.)*
Well . . . there we are.
*(*OCKHAM *looks up, shifting as if the meeting is over. But the* AMBASSADOR *has turned into himself and is staring at his desk.)*
OCKHAM: Well . . .
(The AMBASSADOR *looks up.)*
AMBASSADOR: I lost a son.
CHESNEAU: Yes. I'm sorry, sir.
AMBASSADOR: My son was killed fighting. He died here. Six years ago. *(He looks at* CHESNEAU.*)* No, well, Bob, thanks for the offer. But I don't think we'll be leaving right now.

48. INT. APARTMENT. NIGHT
Darkness. Then BARBARA*'s face, just hit with a streak of light as she unlatches the door.* CHESNEAU *is standing outside on the landing.*
CHESNEAU: Hi, how are you?
(He smiles. She looks at him a moment.)
I wanted to see you.
(She opens the door.)
BARBARA: Come in. The curfew . . .
CHESNEAU: Oh it's all right.
(She closes the door behind him and goes on past him back into the apartment which is darkened, unlit.)
I'm afraid I've been drinking. One or two of the Agency. . . .
(He stands a moment at the door, apologetically, holding a couple of bottles in his hand. She has gone to sit down at the far end of the apartment on a wooden chair.)
Have you been sleeping?
BARBARA: I'm sitting in the dark.
(There is a pause. He moves into the darkened room.)

123

CHESNEAU: It's been very bad. Things are bad lately. There's an airlift out of Danang. Hue gone, Danang going . . .

BARBARA: I heard the World Service tonight.

(He stands a moment. She is not looking at him.)

CHESNEAU: Listen, I'm sorry . . . I've not been coming to see you. I'm sure . . . you must be angry, I know. It's just . . . it gets to be impossible . . .

BARBARA: Why do you behave as if I'm your wife?

CHESNEAU: What?

BARBARA: *(Quietly, with no apparent bitterness)* It's unattractive. Pouring out excuses. 'I'm sorry, darling, I'm drunk . . .' I'm your girlfriend, there's no responsibility. And thank goodness, no need to report.

(CHESNEAU *looks at her a moment, not understanding her mood.)*

CHESNEAU: Barbara, I'm sorry, I felt you'd be angry . . .

BARBARA: Yes, well, I am. Things are coming to an end. That means going into work hasn't been easy. It's not very pleasant, the look people have. Today there was a girl, a teller, she's been working at the bank, I suppose, two years, she came to me to ask if I could help get her out. I said, well, there's a friend of mine . . . *(She looks at him quickly, then away.)* . . . he can get papers, I think.

CHESNEAU: Yeah, it's not . . . it isn't too easy. For the moment we're playing things down.

(He pauses, miserably. BARBARA *is looking down at her hands.)*

I mean, of course I will for a friend of yours, Barbara. We're trying not to let panic set in.

(He goes on, apologetically. She doesn't turn.)

That's why the radio doesn't quite come through with things. All the news of the military defeats. We don't want things to get too conspicuous. People might take to the streets.

BARBARA: Well, I'm sure. You must lie to them. Lying's got you this far.

CHESNEAU: Barbara, you know I have always protested . . .

124

BARBARA: Yes of course . . . *(She turns to him at last.)* You've protested to *me.*
(There is a pause.)
I remember you so many evenings, lying there. A chance to talk about your work. Then you've gone back into the Embassy . . .

CHESNEAU: Barbara . . .

BARBARA: *Done nothing.* And now you're inventing a fresh set of lies. *(She turns away.)* 'Oh whatever we do we mustn't tell the people. Just get the palefaces out of this mess. . . .'

CHESNEAU: That isn't fair. That's not fair to us. The whole thing is just . . . to keep things in hand.
(There is a miserable silence.)

BARBARA: *(Very quietly.)* This girl said to me, 'I know you'll betray us.' I said, 'Oh I don't think that's true.' She said, 'Oh please you mustn't be offended . . .' *(She turns and looks at him.)* '. . . I know what you do is always for the best.'
(She gets up and goes out of the room. In the distance a light comes on and she passes out of sight. CHESNEAU *alone in the room holding his beer. Then* BARBARA's *voice calling through.)*
These people *know.* They know what's happening. The more you lie, the worse it will get.
*(*CHESNEAU *turns slightly.)*

CHESNEAU: We don't know for sure that everything's over.
*(*BARBARA's *face reappears in the doorway.)*

BARBARA: In that case you're the only people who don't.

49. INT. CORRIDOR. DAY
The main corridor in the CIA. Empty. The noise of people at work in the offices. Then after a few seconds the most almighty explosion not far away. The whole corridor shakes. At once people come running, JUDD *first.*

JUDD: Jesus Christ, what the hell is happening?

125

50. INT. UPSTAIRS CORRIDOR. DAY
The AMBASSADOR *appears, hands on hips, furious in the deserted corridor upstairs.*
AMBASSADOR: What the hell is going on here?

51. INT. STAIRWELL. DAY
The enormous stairwell at the centre of the Embassy. The AMBASSADOR *appears on the stairs. Above him, a door is opened at the very top of the well, and an anxious American* MARINE *is seen staring up into the sky. The* AMBASSADOR *yells up from the railing three floors below.*
AMBASSADOR: Soldier, what's happening?
(The MARINE *calls back down.)*
MARINE: There's just one fighter, sir. He's bombing the Presidential Palace, it's like.
(A very loud voice through the whole building, screaming at full pitch.)
VOICE: Hey. Get away from the windows. *Everyone.* Get down on the floor.

52. INT. CORRIDOR. DAY
The corridor now with forty people lying dead-still on the ground, as for a post-nuclear exercise. A pause. Then the whine of an approaching jet and another tremendous explosion. The corridor shakes again. Then the sound of the jet disappearing into the distance. Silence. Nobody moves.
Then the first person sits up.

53. INT. OCKHAM'S OFFICE. DAY
A couple of minutes later. A jump in sound as from outside you can hear people sorting themselves out, calling to one another, as CHESNEAU *comes into the room.* OCKHAM *is already on the phone at his desk, apparently as calm as ever.*
OCKHAM: *(Phone.)* OK. All right.
CHESNEAU: What the hell was that about?
*(*OCKHAM *looks up briefly.)*

126

OCKHAM: *(Phone.)* OK. Yeah. I understand.

CHESNEAU: Jack.

(OCKHAM *nods and puts down the phone.)*

OCKHAM: Some mad pilot. A cowboy. Decided to fight the war on his own.

(He shrugs slightly and turns back to his desk to sit down. JUDD *has come in to join them.)*

What can you do? There's very little damage . . .

CHESNEAU: Nobody knew what the hell was happening. *(He has begun to shout.)* Nobody had any idea how to deal with it.

OCKHAM: No, well, of course.

(He looks at him, very quiet, his calm for the first time seeming unnatural, almost pathological.)

It was a surprise.

(He reaches for a bottle of whisky from a drawer in his desk. CHESNEAU *looks at him, rattled by his elaborate calm.)*

CHESNEAU: Jack, I thought we had radar defences. This town is meant to be ringed. That maniac came clear through the airspace . . .

OCKHAM: Yes, I know.

CHESNEAU: We're just sitting here. *(He looks up to the ceiling.)* When is that mad bastard in that office going to realize we need to get out?

(A pause. OCKHAM *looks at* JUDD, *who is looking at the floor.)*

OCKHAM: Bob, understand you have my permission. If you're unhappy, you're free to resign.

54. EXT. BASEBALL GROUND. DAY

CHESNEAU *stands in the bleachers watching the lunchtime baseball in the Embassy compound.* JUDD *has followed him out.*

CHESNEAU: It's not even me, it's not me I'm thinking of . . .

JUDD: No . . .

CHESNEAU: I don't give a shit what happens to us.

(He sits down on one of the benches and gets out a sandwich. JUDD *sits beside him.)*

127

It's those thousands of people who helped us. We made them a promise. And it's getting too late. The Ambassador dreams of some personal triumph. Ockham moves his furniture out . . .

JUDD: I didn't know that.

CHESNEAU: Sure. *Things.* Joan's cat . . .

(He nods at JOAN *who is approaching them.)*

Objects. Money. Everything but the *people* can go.

*(*JOAN *opens her handbag to give a note to* JUDD. *Inside* CHESNEAU *sees a .45 pistol.)*

New gun, Joan?

MACKINTOSH: I got it in case we ever get caught.

(She smiles at JUDD.*)*

Frank and I . . . we have an agreement. We're going to shoot each other in the head.

(She goes. CHESNEAU *watches her leave, but* JUDD *has turned and is looking at* CHESNEAU, *as if preparing to say something difficult.)*

JUDD: Bob, I've been wanting to say to you, you don't get anywhere by being so awkward.

CHESNEAU: Awkward?

JUDD: Lately you've become very loud. Whether you're right or wrong, it's not very effective. You're not going to make anyone want to change their mind. Jack Ockham, for God's sake, he's as eager to start the evacuation as you are. More eager. But he also knows the way to persuade the Ambassador is never going to be by raising his voice. I'm not quite sure why you do it. What your motives are for this bitterness, Bob. It's self-indulgent. And it doesn't have the effect you require.

(There is a pause.)

I say this from personal friendship.

CHESNEAU: *(Quietly)* Is this what everyone feels?

55. INT. BANK. DAY

The bank besieged with people desperate to trade their piastres. Much argument with tellers. People behind the counters work-

ing flat out. A TELLER *brings a packet to Barbara's desk where she is working.*
TELLER: This has been delivered by hand.
BARBARA: Thank you.
   (The TELLER *goes.* BARBARA *looks at the packet, opens its top, takes the merest second's glance, then gets up and goes over to another of the tellers, a girl of 17 on a high stool. At once* LHAN *gets up and follows* BARBARA *to a small filing office at the side of the main hall.)*
Lhan, come in here. . . .

56. INT. FILING OFFICE. DAY
Continuous. They go in, BARBARA *closing the door, then she takes the packet and empties it out on a small table.*
LHAN: Thank you.
   (Inside the packet are an air ticket and a passport which BARBARA *hands across, as she looks in the ticket.)*
BARBARA: Here's your passport as well.
LHAN: Thank you, Miss Dean.
   *(*LHAN *is delighted. She gestures outside.)*
I have the dollars.
BARBARA: That's all right. You'll need them where you're going. The flight is today. You must leave the bank early.
LHAN: All right.
   (She takes the ticket from BARBARA. *Then pauses.)*
Miss Dean, I have an aunt. Also . . . she has two brothers.
   *(*BARBARA *looks at her a moment, then leans across and kisses her with great affection. Then she leaves the room, but not encouragingly.)*
BARBARA: Leave their names. I'll see what I can do.

57. INT. SHREDDING ROOM. DAY
At once a great noise as OCKHAM *moves down a line of eight paper-shredders which are being fed continuously with thousands of documents, which are being unloaded by teams of assistants. We are in a large filing room, almost like a steel vault, whose contents have been ransacked and poured out on to the*

129

floor. As OCKHAM *moves down the line, assistants come up to
him with individual bundles for his personal approval.*

OCKHAM: Yeah, all that. *(He looks briefly at the next bundle.)*
Get rid of it. *(The next.)* Yeah. Yeah. Sure, that as well. Anything with names we got to get rid of it. *(He speaks even
before the next assistant has reached him.)* If it's got names,
then it must go.

58. INT. INCINERATOR ROOM. DAY

*An inferno of heat and noise. A terrible whine from the ma-
chines. Three men dressed only in trousers are shovelling piles
of shredded paper into the incinerators. There are carts of
shredded paper waiting to go. The fire inside is fierce.* OCKHAM
stands near the men, shouting at the top of his voice to be heard.

OCKHAM: It's hot.

MAN: Yeah. Ventilation. *(He points up to the ceiling.)* I don't
think it's working.

*(*OCKHAM *nods. Then gestures at the great piles of paper.)*

OCKHAM: I'm afraid this is only the beginning. Just keep going
as long as you can.

59. INT. OCKHAM'S OFFICE. DAY

OCKHAM *is now sitting at his desk downstairs. Round the door
appears a very Ivy League State Department* YOUNG MAN, *ner-
vous, in a suit.* OCKHAM *looks up.*

YOUNG MAN: I'm sorry, sir. It's the Ambassador. He says can
you turn the incinerators off?

*(*OCKHAM *frowns.)*

He says he's sorry, but please can you do it?

(The YOUNG MAN *looks nervously at* OCKHAM.*)*

He says the ash is falling on the pool.

60. INT. BANK. NIGHT

QUOC *is sitting alone with the ledgers in the deserted bank. He is
at his desk, in the back area.* BARBARA *appears in front of him,
very still.*

BARBARA: Quoc. I'm afraid I sent Lhan off today.

QUOC: Yes, that's all right. She told me she would go.

(BARBARA *nods slightly.*)

BARBARA: I wanted to ask . . . if you would like me to help you.

QUOC: No.

(There is a pause. QUOC *stares at her impassively.)*

BARBARA: I felt I must ask.

QUOC: Whatever happens, I am staying in my country. My family, my life is here.

BARBARA: But you hate the Communists.

QUOC: No, I don't hate them, I fear them, that's all.

(She looks at him as if about to say something important.)

BARBARA: The bank will trade until the last moment.

QUOC: Yes, of course.

BARBARA: I needed to say . . .

(She stops, unable to express herself. She puts her hand suddenly over her mouth. QUOC *seems simply to wait. She sees this and turns away.)*

Well, I'm sorry, I shouldn't have disturbed you. *(She turns to go.)* Good night, Quoc.

QUOC: Good night, Miss Dean.

61. INT. SITUATION ROOM. NIGHT

A group of senior Embassy men in the situation room. In the DAO's office inside the Embassy. It is late at night. The maps on the walls are dramatically lit by neon. At the centre of the room, surrounded by senior military, the AMBASSADOR *sits in deep gloom.* CHESNEAU *sits near* OCKHAM. *The* OFFICER *at the wall has just finished reporting from a large map of Military Region Three.*

OFFICER: I'm sorry, sir. There is nothing in the military situation which gives any ground for hope. I would say . . . Saigon is encircled. At any moment the attack can be pressed home. *(He waits a moment, then tries to go on.)* In a way, I don't quite know why they're waiting . . .

131

AMBASSADOR: They're waiting because they still want to talk. *(His voice is barely raised.)* Why fight your way in when you can negotiate? They don't want to see this city destroyed. *(There is a silence. He is plainly on his own, yet no one wants to speak.* OCKHAM *leads quietly.)*

OCKHAM: Well, in that case, there's a precondition. Something we've discussed here before. For many years. It is a condition that the North will not negotiate unless President Thieu is removed.

AMBASSADOR: And it is of course I who must do it. *(There is a pause.)* Oh yes, Jack. *I* must hold the knife. *(Everyone looks at him in concealed astonishment. The military stare as he goes on.)* This man who's been loyal to us. A cup of bitterness. And you are all so keen I should drink. *(*OCKHAM *looks down, embarrassed.)*

OCKHAM: Well, it does seem . . . if we want to negotiate . . .

AMBASSADOR: Oh yes, of course, sound reasons I'm sure. *(He gets up from the chair and moves across the room, muttering. Then he turns and faces them.)* Well, so be it. It's what you've always wanted. All of you. Well . . . you have your way. *(He looks down to the floor. There is a silence.)*

CHESNEAU: *(Neutrally, not intimidated)* Does that mean, sir, we can start to evacuate? *(The* AMBASSADOR *turns and looks at him.)*

AMBASSADOR: Oh yes, Chesneau. Let hell come down.

62. INT. BAR. NIGHT

A rundown bar in the centre of town. Behind the bar the TV is on and Thieu is addressing the nation in obviously historic terms. At the bar in a line sit CHESNEAU, JOAN MACKINTOSH, FRANK JUDD *and* BRAD, *a middle-aged American industrialist.*

CHESNEAU *gets down from his stool and passes the television as he goes to the phone. He dials.*
CHESNEAU: Barbara. It's Bob.
BARBARA: *(VO)* Hello.
CHESNEAU: Are you watching?

63. INT. APARTMENT. NIGHT
In Barbara's darkened apartment the trunks have been pulled to the centre of the room, and her belongings are half packed into them. She is sitting on the edge of the bed and in the room distantly you can see the same flickering image on the TV behind her—Thieu in black and white.
BARBARA: Yes. The television's on.
CHESNEAU: *(VO)* The Ambassador went to get rid of him this morning. He still seems to think it's going to help him get talks.
(BARBARA *is staring ahead, detached.*)
BARBARA: Does that mean. . . ?
CHESNEAU: *(VO)* Yeah. We start the big evacuation. All our effort's now to get people out.
(BARBARA *does not react. He goes on with false enthusiasm.*)
(VO) The wraps are really off. It's really beginning.
BARBARA: Ah well, good.
CHESNEAU: *(VO)* Yes. Well, we're pleased.
(Pause. BARBARA waiting. CHESNEAU's voice changes tone.)
(VO) Barbara, are you planning . . . are you going to leave yet?
BARBARA: No. *(She looks down.)* I've nothing. I've no life out there. Also . . . Bob . . . *(Her need is suddenly naked.)* I miss you . . . can we meet?

64. INT. BAR. NIGHT
Continuous. CHESNEAU *stands by the bar, turned away from the others, phone in hand, listening. He pauses a moment.*
CHESNEAU: I'd like to see you. But I have to go to the airport tonight.

133

65. EXT. OCKHAM'S HOUSE. NIGHT
Ockham's house seen from the front in the near darkness, late at night. Just a glint of light on the front steps and into it at once steps a short, beautifully dressed dandy. He stops a moment. It is THIEU. *Then* CHESNEAU's *voice from the dark, tactful.*
CHESNEAU: Sir.
    (Behind THIEU, *unseen in the dark, a couple of bodyguards whisper quietly but urgently.* THIEU *nods and moves down the steps, out of the light. At once we see a black car drawn up in the driveway.* JUDD *holding the back door open. The small figure gets silently into the car.* JUDD *goes round the back and closes the trunk, which is crammed with many fine leather suitcases.* CHESNEAU *is waiting at the passenger door and the two of them get into the seats, slipping in like French gangsters.* CHESNEAU *starts the engine. Then looks in his rear mirror where he can see* THIEU's *face staring straight ahead.)*
CHESNEAU: Sir, if you could . . . if you could just keep down . . .

66. EXT. STREET. NIGHT
The black car moving smoothly through the now silent curfewed streets. The only moving object on a still landscape. As it goes by we see JUDD *and* CHESNEAU, *but the back is apparently empty.*

67. INT. CAR. NIGHT
CHESNEAU *intent on driving, looking around.* JUDD *beside him looks in the mirror, shifts slightly.*
JUDD: *(Quietly)* Are you, em . . . are you going to join your family, sir?
    *(*THIEU's *voice from the floor of the back of the car.)*
THIEU: No. They are buying antiques. *(He nods judiciously, then looks quickly at* CHESNEAU, *alert for trouble from outside.)*
They have already gone to London.

134

(We see THIEU *for the first time. He is sitting on the floor of the car, right down at the back. His two bodyguards are squeezed beside him.* JUDD's *voice.)*

JUDD: *(VO)* London's nice at this time of year.

68. INT. GYMNASIUM. DAY
A wide shot of the huge empty gymnasium which the DOA will use as evacuation headquarters. It is almost empty but for some trestle tables which stand waiting, stacked at the side of the building. Old basketball nets hang from the ceiling.

BARBARA: *(VO)* So it began, the delayed evacuation . . .

69. INT. GYMNASIUM. DAY
FIEDLER *at the centre of the gym. Now teams of marines all around as he describes how he wants everything laid out.*

FIEDLER: Tables . . . Lines of applications . . . Vietnamese exit papers over there . . .
(With each instruction he gestures hugely.)

70. INT. GYMNASIUM. DAY
The scene being transformed. Tables being set up. Men arriving with temporary office equipment. Catering equipment passed hand to hand along a human chain. FIEDLER *on the move, pointing to where everything is to go, receiving attendant soldiers as they come to him for instruction.*

BARBARA: *(VO)* Out at the airport they transformed the gym . . . *(*FIEDLER *points to one corner.)*

FIEDLER: Kitchens. *(Then to a pile of equipment.)* Gas burners. *(He points again.)* Toilet facilities . . .
(A SOLDIER *has come up to him, pointing to a fresh mound of PX goods.)*

SOLDIER: Sir, this is three hundredweight of franks and beans. *(They stand, laughing easily.)*

71. INT. GYMNASIUM. DAY
The scene transformed completely. Tables set out in immaculate rows. Men waiting behind them to receive the lines. Ropes

set out to define the lines. Kitchen staff waiting with gleaming equipment. In the space of a few hours, a perfect logistical operation has been finished, and the team for the job now stands waiting.

BARBARA: *(VO)* They built a facility they called Dodge City.

(FIEDLER *at the centre of the room turns to an attendant officer.)*

FIEDLER: OK, everyone. Open the doors.

PART THREE

72. INT. TAXI. DAY

Fade-up. BARBARA *in the back of a taxi going through the streets of Saigon. They are very crowded. On the sidewalks people are gathering round the street traders, who have huge piles of goods stacked around them.*

BARBARA: *(VO)* The last few days the streets were always busy . . . all the objects people needed to unload . . .

(We watch the sidewalks going by from behind the glass.)

Wherever you went, air-conditioning units . . . fridges . . . televisions . . . stoves . . .

73. INT. APARTMENT. DAY

Barbara's apartment now cleared out. The luggage neatly stacked at the centre of the room. Around the walls and shelves have been cleared. On a rail in the corner of the room there are still a few dresses and BARBARA *is now handing one to her* MAID.

BARBARA: Have this, OK?

MAID: Yes, thank you.

(She holds it up delightedly against her body.)

Hey, it's good, it really looks good . . .

(BARBARA looks at her a moment.)

BARBARA: You know it means that soon I'll be leaving?

MAID: Oh yes.

(The MAID turns with unconcern, and stands delightedly with a mirror.)

Hey, I'm going to look good.

137

SAIGON: YEAR OF THE CAT

74. INT. CERCLE SPORTIF. DAY
BARBARA *in the women's locker room at the Cercle Sportif. It is deserted. Grey ranks of closets. She has opened her locker and is pouring old tennis gear on to the floor.*
BARBARA: *(VO)* Suddenly at last the Cercle Sportif was deserted . . .

75. EXT. CERCLE SPORTIF. DAY
A few solitary Frenchmen in chic costumes sit by the large, slightly green pool with Doric pillars behind. The odd servant brings them iced drinks. They read Le Monde.
BARBARA: *(VO)* Only the French still sit by the pool . . . As if the Americans had only come briefly and the French had never expected they would stay.

76. INT. CERCLE SPORTIF. DAY
BARBARA *sitting alone with a drink, staring out, in the part where we earlier saw them playing cards. A waiter comes across with a bunch of roses. She is suddenly beginning to look old.*
BARBARA: *(VO)* The Foreign Minister I'd played bridge with sent me roses. Later I found out he'd already gone . . .
(She smiles up at the waiter, puts the flowers carelessly aside.)
(VO) Like so many . . . without any warning. The Americans got him away in the night.

77. INT. GYMNASIUM. DAY
The gym, transformed again. Now crammed with evacuees in long lines, some of whom have been sleeping on the spot, waiting for their turn for their applications to be processed. The place is patrolled at the side by GIs in olive drab. JUDD *is pushing his way through the crowd with a short* VIETNAMESE *of about 45, who has an overstuffed suitcase. He is trying to reach* COLONEL FIEDLER *who is still at the centre of things, but by now worn down, frazzled.* JUDD *has to shout to make himself heard.*

138

JUDD: Colonel, I'm wondering . . . This is a friend of mine.
FIEDLER: Everyone seems to have so many friends.
JUDD: He's a tailor. He made shirts for the Embassy.
(FIEDLER *looks at him a moment, then turns to* JUDD.)
FIEDLER: Any idea why he's decided to go?
(JUDD *turns to the* TAILOR *and speaks to him in Vietnamese. As he answers,* JUDD *translates.)*
JUDD: Everyone else is going . . . all his friends have already left.
FIEDLER: Yeah, OK . . .
(He looks at the TAILOR *hopelessly.)*
Well, why not then?
(He reaches across for a couple of exit papers from an officer's pile on a nearby table.)
Tell him he may have to wait for a while.

78. INT. BANK. DAY
The bank as normal, peaceful now, in contrast to the airport. Everything in its familiar place. BARBARA *working at her desk.* QUOC *appears beside her.*
QUOC: Miss Dean, I'm afraid we have lost Mr Haliwell.
BARBARA: What?
(He reaches out with an envelope.)
QUOC: He asked to pass you on this.
(She looks up, then goes and opens the door of Haliwell's office.)

79. INT. OFFICE. DAY
The office is empty. The desk cleared. The ledgers in a tidy pile at the side of the desk. The Times still in its place. A coat hangs on the coat rack. BARBARA *moves into the office, reading the letter.* QUOC *follows her in.*
QUOC: He went for lunch and he left you this message.
BARBARA: Yes.
(She has opened it. Inside there is a note and an airline ticket. She looks at the ticket, then turns as if to resume normality.)

139

Well, thank you, Quoc.

(QUOC *lingers, surprised he is being dismissed.*)

QUOC: Are you leaving?

BARBARA: What?

QUOC: Will you follow him?

(She looks at him a moment.)

BARBARA: What do you think I should do?

(QUOC *raises his eyebrows slightly.*)

QUOC: I would say yes. It will come anyway. Better you do it as soon as you can.

80. INT. BANK. DAY

The back area. Everyone diligently at work, as QUOC *and* BARBARA *come out of Haliwell's office. She makes for the desk, pauses a moment, reaches for the cardigan which is draped round the back of the chair.*

QUOC: No, leave that. It is less suspicious.

(She nods and begins to move away.)

BARBARA: Yes.

QUOC: But your handbag . . . if you want cigarettes . . .

(He is pointing to the bag which is left on the chair. BARBARA *realizes and dips down to pick it up.)*

BARBARA: Yes. Thank you.

QUOC: No. You are welcome.

(They stand looking at each other.)

BARBARA: Goodbye, Quoc.

QUOC: Goodbye, Miss Dean.

81. INT. BANK. DAY

At once a high shot of the bank at work. BARBARA *walking quickly down the stairs and out the main door.*

82. INT. CORRIDOR. DAY

The busy corridor at the CIA Headquarters, fifth floor. CHES-NEAU *is coming down the corridor. He is wearing a helmet, and his hand is stuffed with papers.* JUDD *is coming from the other direction, also in a helmet.*

CHESNEAU: What's the news?

JUDD: There's been a second ultimatum. It says all US personnel must withdraw. . . .

(They keep on moving together towards the offices.)

If we don't get out there's going to be bloodshed . . . *(He turns back ironically.)* The Ambassador says they still want to talk.

83. INT. OFFICE. DAY

The office is as busy as ever, but all the secretaries who are otherwise dressed normally are wearing helmets. The effect is very odd. As soon as she sees him coming through, LINDA *gets up to talk to* CHESNEAU, *who is coming in talking to* JUDD.

CHESNEAU: *And* we're expecting an attack on the airport . . .

LINDA: Bob . . .

*(*CHESNEAU *nods to* JUDD *that he'll join him in a minute, recognizing the seriousness of* LINDA's *tone. She silently nods him over to the quiet corner of the office. They go to a filing cabinet which has a Thomson sub-machine-gun lying incongruously on top of it.)*

There's a woman downstairs.

*(*CHESNEAU *frowns.)*

The woman who came with you . . .

CHESNEAU: Ah yes.

(He stands a moment, not knowing what to do.)

LINDA: . . . last Christmas . . .

(He nods.)

CHESNEAU: Put her in a room. I'll be down when I can.

84. INT. EMBASSY. DAY

BARBARA *is walked down the ground-floor passage of the Embassy by two Marines. They open a door, and inside is a deserted office, which has been cleared. It is empty.* BARBARA *goes in. The*

141

walls are decorated by pictures of America, posters of the Rockies, Manhattan, etc.

BARBARA: Thank you.

(The two men go, closing the door. She sits down, alone.)

85. INT. BANK. DAY

QUOC *sitting at his desk, as usual. The work of the bank going on. A couple of tellers laughing, during the slack period. Then a third teller signals to* QUOC *to come over. A young* AMERICAN WOMAN *is at the other side of the counter.*

WOMAN: I'm so sorry. I need my credit cleared. Is the manager here?

QUOC: Yes of course. I'll just speak to him. *(He reaches through the guichet and takes her cheque book.)* Will you hold on a moment, please?

(We see him walk into the manager's office, having tapped three times on the door. He goes in. A pause. The tellers chatter, oblivious. Then after a few moments he comes out again, closing the door behind him. He rejoins the tellers and customer.)

The manager says, yes, we can pay on this. *(He pushes the book back.)* Would you like to make out your cheque?

86. EXT. EMBASSY. NIGHT

The American Embassy seen from outside. The huge white building. The night is silent around it, but high in the building lights burn.

87. INT. OCKHAM'S OFFICE. NIGHT

A very low-key briefing, dead of night. OCKHAM *at his desk, the few trusted analysts around the room.* OCKHAM *tired. There are cans of Heineken on his desk.*

OCKHAM: The North is going to give us twenty-four hours. It's been negotiated. That's how long they're willing to hold off.

Washington is insisting no phoney heroics. We are only to take essential locals with us at the end.

CHESNEAU: What does that mean?

OCKHAM: It means what we want it to, Bob. *(He smiles, bitterly.)* They've never known anything of what it's like here. *(He looks down, uncharacteristically emotional.)* Meanwhile please . . . your work is nearly over. I'd advise you all to try and get some sleep.

88. INT. EMBASSY. NIGHT

BARBARA *asleep in a chair in the Embassy office.* CHESNEAU *standing over her in the near dark. She looks abandoned.* CHESNEAU *speaks to her asleep.*

CHESNEAU: I'm sorry, I was working.

(She wakes. Looks at him. Smiles.)

BARBARA: What?

CHESNEAU: I didn't forget you.

BARBARA: I couldn't face leaving.

CHESNEAU: No, it's all right.

BARBARA: Haliwell went . . .

CHESNEAU: In that case he must have caught the last plane.

(CHESNEAU *moves away.*)

The airport's gone.

(BARBARA *in real panic looks across at him.*)

BARBARA: Oh Bob, have I been very stupid?

CHESNEAU: No. You can helicopter out. The Jolly Green Giants. We're bringing them into downtown Saigon.

(BARBARA *looks at him, puzzled.*)

BARBARA: But how do you know. . . ?

CHESNEAU: There's an agreement. They're giving us exactly twenty-four hours. And everyone's ready. All American citizens have been issued with assembly points. *(He smiles.)* They're waiting for a signal.

(BARBARA *smiles also, in anticipation.*)

BARBARA: You play 'White Christmas'?

CHESNEAU: Yes. They're serious.

143

BARBARA: I thought it was a joke.

CHESNEAU: It's a joke. It's serious as well.

(They smile at each other, the old humour between them, the old tone of voice.)

The radio station plays Bing Crosby, and all Americans know it's the end.

89. EXT. EMBASSY COMPOUND. NIGHT

The empty compound outside the Embassy streaked with searchlights which are now on for the night. The noise of gun-fire has now died. From the dark, running very lightly, come two GIs *and an* OFFICER, *making for a huge tree which dominates the compound. One* GI *stumbles slightly as he reaches it.*

FIRST GI: Shit.

OFFICER: Keep it quiet.

SECOND GI: How the hell. . . ? *(He gestures despairingly at the huge chainsaw he is carrying.)* There's no way he ain't going to hear it.

OFFICER: It's the Ambassador's favourite tree.

(The FIRST GI *makes a signal of despair and looks up at the great branches of the tamarind. The* OFFICER *shrugs.)*

We've gotta do it. We need the landing space. *(He nods at the* SECOND GI.*)* Nothing for it. Let's go.

(The two men start the chainsaw. The petrol motor is deafening.)

Jesus.

(It bites into the trunk. At once, at a high window, way up on the top floor of the Embassy, the stricken figure of the AMBASSADOR *appears, like a prisoner shouting from behind his bullet-proof glass.)*

AMBASSADOR: What the hell is going on here?

90. INT. APARTMENT. DAY

There are some bags, packed, in the centre of the room. CHESNEAU *stands alone in the living room. He is looking at his*

144

watch. It says 7:45. BARBARA *is out of sight, gathering stuff from the bedroom. She calls to him from there.*

BARBARA: *(VO)* Nearly ready.

CHESNEAU: It's OK.

BARBARA: *(VO)* I'm sorry, I'm taking your time up.

CHESNEAU: No. *(He stands, patient. Then almost to himself)* Go your own speed.

(For the first time BARBARA *appears, by the door jamb. She holds a few random objects she is planning to pack.)*

BARBARA: Do you want to go?

CHESNEAU: Yeah, there'll be choppers at the Embassy.

BARBARA: And what . . . you think I should get on?

CHESNEAU: Well sure, I mean . . .

BARBARA: No I meant . . . you mean *now?* Or can't I hang on for you?

(A pause, he does not reply.)

I've never even asked where the helicopter takes me.

CHESNEAU: To the Philippines.

(He smiles slightly, but already she is going on with a new urgency.)

BARBARA: Listen, I have a friend. A terrific girl. She used to bring me laundry. Put her on. She's a wonderful girl. Let her go in my place.

(He is still looking at her.)

Why not? Just the chance to be with you.

(She turns away.)

It's the waste. All the time we've wasted.

CHESNEAU: Yes, I know. That was my fault.

(He moves across the room. She is in his arms.)

When I first came here, Barbara, I thought I could do this job decently. I thought it was honourable work. And even now I'm not ashamed, all the work we've done, this week, all the people I've managed to get out. But also it's the nature of the thing. It's been left to us. 'Hey, you guys, go and make us look good.' Well, we didn't. We weren't any better at losing the war than we were at winning it. And Barbara . . . you made it worse for me. Every time I saw you, you made me feel guilty. I couldn't take that after a while. That's why I stopped coming to see you. *(Tenderly)* Now it seems stupid. Now that we're here.

(They embrace. There is a pause.)

BARBARA: It's so strange. Everywhere you go you hear people saying 'Oh I loved this country.' That what they say. They usually say it just as they're leaving. 'Oh I loved this country so much . . .' I realized when I was in the bank one evening. This was . . . oh some time ago. I tried to say something affectionate to Quoc. Well, that's what you're left with. Gestures of affection. Which you then find mean nothing at all.

CHESNEAU: *(Moved)* Barbara, please . . .

(But she at once moves past him, leaving the room.)

BARBARA: Put me on a helicopter!

CHESNEAU: Barbara . . .

BARBARA: Shut up! Put me on!

(She leaves the room. A silence. CHESNEAU, left alone, stunned by this sudden change.

We cut to BARBARA in the bathroom. She is putting her toilet things into a sponge bag. CHESNEAU appears behind her at the door.)

CHESNEAU: What will you do? Will you go back to England?

BARBARA: My mother.

CHESNEAU: May I come and see you there?

(She turns and looks at him as if the idea were self-evidently absurd. Then she quietly tips the cosmetics into the sink and leaves them behind.)

BARBARA: I think let's leave the place to be looted. Don't you think so?

(She goes from the bathroom. She goes from the main room, leaving her bag behind on the floor.)

CHESNEAU: Sure, if you want.

A Map of the World, The Public Theatre, New York City, 1985

Roshan Seth, Elizabeth McGovern

A Map of the World, The Public Theatre, New York City, 1985

Zeljko Ivanek, Roshan Seth, Alfre Woodard, Elizabeth McGovern

SAIGON: YEAR OF THE CAT

91. EXT. STREET. DAY

CHESNEAU *comes quickly down the stairs carrying Barbara's luggage urgently now to the car. As he puts it down he looks up into the sky, and we cut to the helicopters arriving overhead. Marine helicopters are now flying overhead into the city.* CHESNEAU *and* BARBARA *drive together through the streets. As they pass along a shopping street, they see the old South Vietnamese flags being pulled down, and the flags of the new regime being put up.*

As their car draws closer to the Embassy, they overtake straggling lines of Americans who are walking with their suitcases down the road towards the compound.

92. INT. CAR. DAY

Inside the car the radio is playing 'White Christmas' as BARBARA *watches the stragglers in the street.*

BARBARA: Look! Coming in on signal . . .

(CHESNEAU *smiles. The crowd begins to thicken as they approach the Embassy. They pass burning and wrecked-out cars. As they get near the gate they see a huge crowd.* BARBARA *points to the thickest part.*)

Look! Over there!

93. EXT. EMBASSY GATE. DAY

Outside the Embassy in the huge crowd, HALIWELL *is desperately trying to push his way through. He is carrying a suitcase, lost in a hostile crowd.*

HALIWELL: English! English! Please I'm English! English! Please let me through!

94. INT. CAR. DAY

BARBARA *desperately trying to catch sight of him through the crowd.*

CHESNEAU *trying to edge the car towards him through the crowd, who are now beginning to turn ugly. They bang on the roof. They hit the side of the car with their fists.*

147

BARBARA: He must have got caught at the airport.
CHESNEAU: Hold on. Let me try . . .

95. EXT. STREET. DAY
The first great helicopter hovers over the Embassy to make its way down into the compound. At once the crowd begins to push even harder, packing in a press towards the gate.
HALIWELL: English! English!
(In the excitement he is pushed to the ground. Some random rifle shots are fired in the air. People scream. CHESNEAU *draws alongside* HALIWELL.)
CHESNEAU: Quick. Get him in.
*(*BARBARA *reaches for the door and opens it, as* CHESNEAU *stretches right across the seats and pulls* HALIWELL *like a beached whale into the car. He turns back to the wheel, while* BARBARA *closes the door.)*
HALIWELL: My God!
CHESNEAU: Close the door!
*(*BARBARA *slams it as the car is inched towards the gates.)*
HALIWELL: Oh God, for a moment out there . . .
(He stops, checking himself, BARBARA *looks at him. He tries to smile and shake his head. The gate is opened fractionally to allow Chesneau's car into the compound.)*
CHESNEAU: Right, OK. We're getting there.
(We watch the crowd surging against the gate, the GIs *holding them back with rifles.)*
BARBARA: For a moment you felt what it's like to be them.

96. EXT. COMPOUND. DAY
The tremendous circular cloud of dust going up as the first helicopter comes down with a great roar by the tree stump. Marines jump from the helicopter with guns as it lands. The crowd inside the compound, half white, half Asian, gathers round to get on. The GI *is shouting above the noise.*
FIRST GI: It's all right. Everyone's going. Please. Everyone. Just hold on.

(By the gate the far greater crowd is pressing much more urgently to get in. A man now flings himself at the gate in an attempt to climb over. At once a GI *brings his rifle butt crashing down on his head.*

We cut back to the GI *inside the compound.)*

Everyone OK. There will be a place for you. Everyone inside is going to get on.

97. INT. CORRIDOR. DAY

COLONEL FIEDLER *walking along the main corridor in fatigues and helmet. It is absolute chaos. The place has been ransacked as fast as possible to destroy as much equipment and papers as possible. People are running back and forth with stuff for the incinerators. The* COLONEL *is simply opening the door of each room and shouting inside.*

COLONEL: All right, please, let's get on with it. Everyone out. We're all going home.

(He comes into the communal office, now ravaged by the speed of the exit. LINDA *and the others are still working in helmets, piling stuff out of cabinets on to the floor.)*

All women first. Hey—

(He smiles at LINDA. *The mood is good-hearted.)*

Out please. *(Then a military joke.)* Everyone, please, in orderly lines.

98. INT. PASSAGEWAY. DAY

At the end of a concrete passageway you can see teams of people, about forty in all, feeding papers into the burners in the distance. They are scorched with effort. At the front there is a SOLDIER *hauling a big bag along, single-handed. He is stopped by an* OFFICER.

OFFICER: Soldier, what's that?

SOLDIER: It's two million dollars, sir.

(The OFFICER *looks at him.)*

It's the Ambassador's emergency fund.

OFFICER: Where's it going?

149

SAIGON: YEAR OF THE CAT

SOLDIER: I've orders to burn it.
(The OFFICER *nods, and casually reaches into the bag, takes out a handful of dollars and stuffs them into the* MAN's *hand.)*
OFFICER: All right, soldier. I'll see to that.

99. EXT. COMPOUND. DAY
The crowd gathered at the helicopter. We watch the COMMANDING OFFICER *at work, striding round the area.*
COMMANDING OFFICER: OK here, please. Yeah. You here. OK, yeah.
(The MARINE *inside the helicopter yells across.)*
MARINE: That's all we can take.
*(*CHESNEAU *appears at the* OFFICER's *side.)*
CHESNEAU: Bill, I've two friends.
OFFICER: Sure, put 'em on then.
*(*CHESNEAU *turns back. At the front of the crowd,* BARBARA *and* HALIWELL *are standing together.)*
CHESNEAU: Barbara!
(They make their way past the crowd to the helicopter. HALIWELL *gets on.* CHESNEAU *holds a moment with* BARBARA.)*
Good luck, OK?
(As they stand looking, the OFFICER *passes them impatiently.)*
OFFICER: Come on, please.
(And CHESNEAU *steps back, yells to the helicopter.)*
CHESNEAU: Goodbye, Mr Haliwell.
BARBARA: God, have I really got to get on to this thing?
(She is muttering to herself as she makes her way. CHESNEAU *waves to* HALIWELL *inside.)*
OFFICER: OK, everyone, please—let's lift it.
(The crowd falls back.)
Stand by. Everyone clear.
(She is sitting opposite the open main door of the helicopter, next to HALIWELL, *as it begins to go up. She is wearing a*

panama hat. She is an old English spinster. The image rises into the air and out of the frame as we hear the voice of the OFFICER.)

Next lot, OK? Right. Get ready. You. You and you, right? Right. Over there.

100. INT. OFFICE. DAY

CHESNEAU *with an axe is now attacking the laminated maps on the walls of his office. They are absolutely covered with the red scrawls of the advancing army. He is making wild swings to cut the wood they are mounted on. Systematically taking his own anger out.* JUDD *arrives, alarmed by the noise.*

JUDD: God almighty, what the hell are you doing?

(CHESNEAU *turns smiling.*)

CHESNEAU: How do you suggest I get rid of these things?

JUDD: If we had any sense, we'd just set fire to it, we'd burn the whole place down.

(He turns hopelessly to survey the amount of paper still left in the office. CHESNEAU *has pulled the drawer out of a filing cabinet. It is full of plastic individual name cards, several thousand. Each with a person's name on it.)*

CHESNEAU: What about these? People's name plates . . . agents who worked for us. . . .

(From the drawer he also takes duplicated foolscap sheets, all with lists of names.)

Lists. All the people we promised to get out . . .

(OCKHAM *appears at the door.*)

OCKHAM: Oh Bob, could you come?

CHESNEAU: Yeah . . .

(OCKHAM *waves airily as he goes.*)

OCKHAM: Just leave that. . . .

(As he goes out the main office, CHESNEAU *sets the drawer full of names and lists down on a desk.)*

We've got problems with helicopter sites.

(They go out. We pause a moment on the drawer CHESNEAU *has abandoned on the desktop.)*

151

101. EXT. EMBASSY. DAY

A line of people being passed hand to hand up a dangerous chain that leads to the very top of the Embassy where a COMPOUND OFFICER *then handles them into the helicopter on top. Next to him is the* OFFICER *with two million dollars. They shout.*

BAG OFFICER: This doesn't look good.

COMMANDING OFFICER: The ground's too dangerous.

  (He points down to the compound where the crowd are now looking up towards the roof. Around them the gates are still besieged.)

We got frightened of killing the gooks.

  *(*BAG OFFICER *nods. And then he puts his hand on the* COMPOUND OFFICER*'s shoulder, as he steps into the line to leave. The* COMPOUND OFFICER *frowns slightly at the size of his bag.)*

You taking that?

BAG OFFICER: Yeah, I have to.

  (The COMPOUND OFFICER *moves round to signal to the pilot.)*

COMPOUND OFFICER: OK. Right. Lift away.

  (He holds both thumbs up. In an immensely precarious movement, the Green Giant lifts off. As it does, it tilts to one side. We just catch sight of the BAG OFFICER, *desperately grabbing at the bag as it slides across the floor. As the helicopter gains height, the bag falls. Thousands and thousands of dollars flutter out of the air.*
  The crowd in the compound looks up as the money flutters down on them and into the pool.)

102. INT. SCHOOL. EVENING

A Vietnamese schoolroom. Two hundred people sitting patiently on the classroom floor with their baggage, while in the headmaster's small office off the main room, an American in late middle age is sitting on the table with a telephone. We recognize him from the Tu Do bar earlier. He has a saddlebag.

As he speaks he looks to the crowds, cramped and patient on the floor.

BRAD: Jack, it's Brad.

OCKHAM: *(VO)* Yeah.

BRAD: Brad at Forbes Chemicals.

OCKHAM: *(VO)* Yeah, I know who you are.

BRAD: I'm with my designated employees. Jack, we've been waiting six hours.

(He looks out to the playground which is cleared and empty, as if waiting for a landing.)

We're at our assembly point, but nobody's come for us. All the choppers are flying right by.

(There's a slight pause at the other end.)

OCKHAM: Yeah, that's right. They're on their way to you.

BRAD: We've decided to make it through town. I'm going to lead them across to the Embassy . . .

OCKHAM: *(VO)* No, please, Brad. . . .

103. INT. OCKHAM'S OFFICE. EVENING

Continuous. OCKHAM *exhausted at his desk. His office is ravaged. The contents have been cleared by Marines who are still working to take things out. The remains of the CIA corps, who number about eight, are working around him on the phones ringing in the offices. There is a great deal of drink—a crate of Heineken at the centre of the room.*

OCKHAM: It's not a good idea.

BRAD: *(VO)* But, Jack . . .

OCKHAM: If you just hold on, we will come and get you. . . .

(He turns and looks at JUDD *who is talking on another phone.)*

The crowd's getting ugly, you must stay where you are.

JUDD: *(Simultaneously)* No, they're coming, I promise you . . .

*(*CHESNEAU *drops a scrawled note across the desk to* JUDD.)

CHESNEAU: Another two hundred waiting in Cholon.

*(*JUDD *sees it but does not acknowledge it. Instead he picks up in his other hand a phone which is ringing and, while he*

153

talks to the first source, cuts the second phone off by pressing down on the cradle.)
JUDD: It's OK. You will be collected.
(Then he drops the newly dead line into the waste-paper basket.)
Nobody is going to get left behind.

104. INT. BANK. NIGHT
QUOC *alone in the bank, closing the shutters with the long pole. It is eerily dark and quiet. Then he walks back across the deserted bank and picks up his briefcase which he puts under his arm. Then he goes to the door and, without looking back, goes out.*

105. INT. WASHROOM. NIGHT
The AMBASSADOR *stands washing his hands, then dries them carefully and walks out of the washroom into the deserted corridor.*

106. INT. CORRIDOR. NIGHT
He walks along the corridor and goes into his office. The corridor is deserted.

107. INT. OFFICE. NIGHT
He walks through his outer office which is now unmanned and goes into his own inner office. It is similarly deserted. He goes to the American flag which is pinned on the wall and now unpins it. He takes it from the wall and folds it into the shape of a tea towel. Then he puts it in a plastic bag which he has left on his desk. He then picks up a cable from his desk and with the bag and the cable leaves the room.

108. INT. CORRIDOR. NIGHT
The corridor which only a moment ago was deserted is now full of the remaining staff who number about twelve in all. They have appeared while the AMBASSADOR *has been in his office and*

are now waiting for him in the corridor. He is haggard, he has flu, he looks terrible. He reads them the cable.

AMBASSADOR: Gentlemen. This is from the President. The Ambassador is ordered to leave. *(He looks down.)* We are withdrawing the American presence under orders. *(He nods slightly and looks at them.)* Thanks very much.

109. INT. CORRIDOR. NIGHT

The whole group seemingly driven along the corridor by the stricken giant at their head. They keep close together as they walk through the darkened building. OCKHAM *and* CHESNEAU *are at the back like straggling schoolboys who can't keep up on the walk. They whisper furiously to one another.*

CHESNEAU: What's going to happen to all those people?

OCKHAM: Bob, there's nothing . . .

CHESNEAU: There are thousands of them still at the assembly points. I tell you, they've been waiting all day.

OCKHAM: We can't, there's nothing . . . *(There is a strange bump and clink in their progress.)*
Shit.

CHESNEAU: What's that?

OCKHAM: Whisky bottle.
(A bottle has rolled out on to the floor from Ockham's pocket, but they do not stop to pick it up. It is left there.)
Face it, Bob. There's nothing we can do.

110. INT. CHESNEAU'S OFFICE. NIGHT

The group go past the open office door. We just catch their voices as they do.

CHESNEAU: But Jack . . . listen. . . .
*(A pause. The office ransacked, deserted. Then we adjust to settle in the foreground on the drawer full of agents' name plates, forgotten on the desk.
We hold on that.)*

155

111. INT. STAIRWELL. NIGHT
At the top landing as the group all reach it, the military are waiting already by the exit door at the top of the building to take the AMBASSADOR *out on the last flight.*
As the group reaches the small landing, the AMBASSADOR *turns to speak to the assembled company. He still holds his bag.*
AMBASSADOR: Gentlemen, before I leave I would like to . . .
    (A great cry from the bottom of the stairwell.)
SOLDIER: Sir. Sir. Let's get the hell out.
    (The AMBASSADOR *shocked by the voice of the panicking* SOLDIER.)
They're breaking into the Embassy.
AMBASSADOR: What?
SOLDIER: They've heard this is going to be the last flight.
    (There is a second's indecision on the AMBASSADOR'*s face, then suddenly he gestures at the door.)*
AMBASSADOR: All right—out!

112. INT. EMBASSY. NIGHT
At once the mad scramble is shown going on downstairs as the two GIs *on guard desperately close the main doors to the Embassy against the crowd. Then they run across the lobby to where a third* GI *is waiting holding the door to the stairway open.*
FIRST GI: OK, for fuck's sake lock it.
    (The main doors being smashed open and the crowd pouring into the Embassy.)

113. INT. STAIRWELL. NIGHT
At the top of the stairwell, the military and CIA scramble desperately out of the tiny exit door on the landing out to the waiting helicopter.

114. INT. STAIRWELL. NIGHT
One GI *slamming the stairwell door and locking it while the other two run for the stairs.*

156

115. EXT. ROOF. NIGHT
*The waiting helicopters now loaded, waiting, blades turning.
The door to the stairwell held open by the last* OFFICER.

116. INT. STAIRWELL. NIGHT
The last SOLDIERS *running up the stairs. Reaching the top.
There are sounds of people coming up from below, but at once
the* GIs *open gas canisters and throw them down the stairs at the
approaching crowd. You catch a glimpse of them scampering
through the door and it closing as the screen smokes out.*

117. EXT. STREETS. NIGHT
*The streets of Saigon. Night. Quiet. Nothing moves. Eerie. The
sound of the helicopters has gone. The cathedral. The opera
house. Tu Do deserted.*

118. EXT. COMPOUND. NIGHT
The two hundred Vietnamese and BRAD *in the school compound, waiting, scanning the empty sky.*

119. EXT. STREETS. NIGHT
*A side street. Round the corner, jogging in a small group, come
eight soldiers in formation. They are in army uniform, with
guns, in full battledress. As they turn into the street, the group
suddenly breaks up and they stop. They put down their guns,
and start to undress. They put down their boots, guns, clothes,
in small heaps on the pavement. They stand a moment in their
boxer shorts. Then turn, as casually as they can, and disappear
down the street. The little puddles of clothes left behind them.*

120. INT. HELICOPTER. NIGHT
*Inside the helicopter the group has settled, cheerful. A false
exhilaration.* CHESNEAU *is sitting next to* JUDD, *on one side.
Suddenly he remembers.*
CHESNEAU: Shit.
JUDD: What?

157

CHESNEAU: I've remembered . . .
(JUDD *puzzled.*)
JUDD: What?
(CHESNEAU *looks down, appalled, disturbed. Avoids the question.*)
CHESNEAU: Something.
JUDD: *(A joke)* Do you want to go back?
(CHESNEAU *turns, looks back, the truth drawing on him of what he has done.*)
CHESNEAU: *(Under his breath)* God forgive us.
(Suddenly the PILOT *turns and yells back from the controls, as a can of Heineken is opened in front of him.)*
PILOT: Hey, you guys. We're all going home!
(Fast fade.)

A MAP OF THE WORLD

A map of the world that does not include Utopia is not worth even glancing at, for it leaves out the one country at which Humanity is always landing. And when Humanity lands there, it looks out, and, seeing a better country, sets sail.

OSCAR WILDE
'The Soul of Man Under Socialism'

A Map of the World was first performed in London at the Lyttelton Theatre on 27 January 1983. The cast was as follows:

ELAINE LE FANU	Sheila Scott-Wilkinson
STEPHEN ANDREWS	Bill Nighy
VICTOR MEHTA	Roshan Seth
PEGGY WHITTON	Diana Quick
ANGELIS	Stefan Gryff
MARTINSON	Ronald Hines
M'BENGUE	John Matshikiza
SCRIPT GIRL	Kate Saunders
MAKE-UP GIRL	Judith Hepburn
PROPMAN	Lilla Towner-Jones
PAUL	Tim Charrington
1ST WAITER	Bhasker
2ND WAITER	Andrew Johnson
3RD WAITER	Nizwar Karanj
DIPLOMATS	Brian Spink
	Jeremy Anthony
	Niven Boyd
BOOM OPERATOR	Bill Moody
SOUND RECORDIST	Robert Phillips
Director	David Hare
Designer	Hayden Griffin
Music	Nick Bicât
Lighting	Rory Dempster

CHARACTERS

ELAINE LE FANU
STEPHEN ANDREWS
VICTOR MEHTA
PEGGY WHITTON
ANGELIS
MARTINSON
M'BENGUE

WAITERS
CREW
ASSISTANTS
DIPLOMATS
ETC

ACT ONE

SCENE ONE. *A hotel lounge. Crumbling grandeur. Cane chairs. A great expanse of black and white checked floor stretching back into the distance. Porticos. Windows at the back and, to one side, oak doors. But the scene must only be sketched in, not realistically complete.*
STEPHEN *is sitting alone, surrounded by international newspapers, which he is reading. He is in his late twenties, but still boyish: tall, thin, dry. He is wearing seersucker trousers, and his jacket is over the chair. He has a now-emptied glass of beer and a bottle beside him. He is English.*
ELAINE *comes through the oak doors, sheets of Gestetnered material in her hand. She is about thirty-five, disarmingly smart and well dressed. Her elegance seems not at all ruffled by the heat. She is a black American.*

ELAINE: The heat.
STEPHEN: I know.
   (ELAINE *goes to the back to look in vain for a waiter.)*
   Are they still talking?
ELAINE: Yes.
STEPHEN: Ah.
ELAINE: The Senegalese delegate is just about to start. *(She wanders back down, nodding at one of his magazines)* Is that *Newsweek?*
STEPHEN: Yes. There's nothing about us. *(He has picked it up and now reads from it)* 'Tracy Underling of Dayton, Ohio, has the rest of her downtown, largely Catholic Santa Maria College class in thrall with the size of her exceptional IQ, which local psycho-expert Lorne Schlitz claims tops genius level at

163

175. Says the bearded Schlitz: "Proof of her abundant intelligence is that she has already begun writing her third novel at the age of five." Subject of the novel will be the life of Mary Tyler Moore . . .'

(ELAINE *smiles and walks away.*)

ELAINE: America!

STEPHEN: I mean, who actually writes this stuff?

ELAINE: Is it any worse than ours?

(STEPHEN *smiles slightly.*)

That M'Bengue is appalling.

STEPHEN: Who?

ELAINE: The Senegalese. He's raising his third point of order.

STEPHEN: It's a compulsion . . .

ELAINE: Yes.

STEPHEN: . . . I'm afraid.

(ELAINE, *at the back, has a sudden burst of impatience.*)

ELAINE: *Why* are there no waiters?

STEPHEN: Because the bar is nowhere near the lounge. In India no bar is anywhere near any lounge in order that five people may be employed to go backwards and forwards between where the drinkers are and where the drink is. Thus the creation of four unnecessary jobs. Thus the creation of what is called a high-labour economy. Thus low wages. Thus the perpetuation of poverty. Thus going screaming out of your head at the incredible obstinacy of the people. *(He shouts)* Waiter!

ELAINE: You'll get used to it.

(STEPHEN *looks across at* ELAINE *who has sat down and is flicking through a magazine. But she seems unconcerned.*)

STEPHEN: I had a friend who rang me and said, 'Is your hotel in a bad area?' I said, 'Well, quite bad.' She said, 'Does it have corpses?' I said, 'Well, no.' She said, 'Well, mine actually has corpses.' And she was right. When I went to see her, there are people who sleep on the pavement . . . who have failed to wake . . . who are just lying there with rats running over them . . .

ELAINE: Bombay's quite prosperous.

STEPHEN: I know. I know. It's a thriving, commercial city of two million people. Only there happen to be seven million people living there, which leaves the extra five million looking pretty stupid every night.

ELAINE: All right.

STEPHEN: Well.

ELAINE: If you want to make a speech, go and give it in there. *(He looks across at her. She has gone back to reading.)*

STEPHEN: I would if I could be heard among the clamour of voices. Is there not something ludicrous in holding an international conference on poverty in these spectacular surroundings, when all we would actually have to do is to take one step into the street to see exactly what the problems of poverty are?

ELAINE: Most of the delegates have.

STEPHEN: Then why is their interest entirely in striking attitudes and making procedural points?

ELAINE: Because that's politics.

STEPHEN: You accept that?

ELAINE: Of course.

STEPHEN: *(His voice rising)* When even now out in the streets . . .

ELAINE: It's the dirt that disgusts you, that's all.

STEPHEN: What?

(ELAINE has put her magazine aside, suddenly deciding to take him on.)

ELAINE: I've watched you the last couple of days . . .

STEPHEN: I see.

ELAINE: . . . since we met. You're like everyone. You can't understand why the peasants should choose to leave the countryside, where they can die a nice clean death from starvation, to come and grub around in the filthy gutter, where they do, however, have some small chance of life.

STEPHEN: That's not quite true.

ELAINE: It shocks you that people prefer to live in cardboard, they prefer to live in excrement, in filth, than go back and die

165

on the land. But they do. And as you want drama, and as this is
your third day in India . . .

STEPHEN: Fourth.

ELAINE: . . . you're determined to find this bad. Because you
come from the West and are absolutely set on having an
experience, so you find it necessary to dramatize. You come
absolutely determined in advance to find India shocking, and
so you can't see that underneath it all there is a great deal
about the life here which isn't too bad. *(She turns back. Quietly)* At least, if you'd covered Vietnam, that's how you'd feel.
(STEPHEN *looks at her a moment.)*

STEPHEN: No, well, of course, I'm not an old hand . . .

ELAINE: No.

STEPHEN: I don't move in your elevated circles. The élite of
foreign correspondents . . .

ELAINE: Quite.

STEPHEN: I'm just a journalist from England on a literary left-
wing magazine . . .

ELAINE: That's right.

STEPHEN: I've never filed stories under fire, or got the natives
to shoot my copy in fluted arrows through the jungle, so of
course I don't have your lofty overview . . .

ELAINE: It's just that I can't stand to listen to people making
value judgements about other people's ways of life. The hip-
popotamus may be perfectly happy in the mud.

STEPHEN: And the Indian, I suppose you think, is perfectly
happy rolling about in excrement.

ELAINE: No, I didn't say that.

STEPHEN: Well.

ELAINE: But it is arrogant to look at the world . . .

STEPHEN: I'm not.

ELAINE: . . . through one particular perspective . . .

STEPHEN: All right.

ELAINE: . . . which is always to say 'This is like the West. This is
not like the West.' What arrogance!

STEPHEN: No, well, I can't see that . . .

166

ELAINE: If I may say . . . I'm sorry. God, this conference.

STEPHEN: I know.

(There is a pause.)

Waiter!

(ELAINE *smiles.)*

It makes you so ill-tempered. You think you'll go for a stroll. 'I wouldn't leave the hotel if I were you, sir,' they say. 'The monsoon is coming.' With a great grin appearing on their faces as if the thought of it just suited them fine. 'Ah, good, the monsoon.' And you caught in it the best of all. I suppose it's the only revenge the poor have, that their land is uninhabitable by anyone but themselves. That we can't drink their water, or eat their food, or walk in their streets without getting mobbed, or endure their weather, or even, in fact, if we are truthful, contemplate their lives . . .

ELAINE: Stephen . . . *(She smiles)* You exaggerate again.

(At the opposite side to the conference hall VICTOR MEHTA *has appeared. He is in his early forties. He is wearing a light brown suit and tie and he has thick black hair. He is an Indian, but his manners are distinctly European.)*

MEHTA: This is UNESCO?

STEPHEN: Yes. The conference on poverty.

MEHTA: Ah.

(MEHTA *turns at once and summons a white-coated boy from off-stage.)* Waiter.

WAITER: Sahib?

MEHTA: Can you see my bags are taken to my room?

WAITER: Boy!

STEPHEN: Ah, you found a waiter.

MEHTA: Certainly. There is no problem, is there?

(TWO WAITERS *appear. They argue with the* FIRST WAITER *in Hindi. The* FIRST WAITER *dismisses them.* MEHTA *turns back to the* WAITER.) And bring me a bottle of white wine. Is there a Pouilly Fuissé?

WAITER: Pouilly Fumé, sir.

MEHTA: Then I will drink champagne.

(The WAITER *goes. The three of them stand a moment. A chilly smile from* MEHTA.*)*

So. Off the plane I enjoy refreshments. Will you join me?

STEPHEN: Of course. But I think they may be expecting you in the conference.

MEHTA: Let them wait.

*(*STEPHEN *is a little surprised, then hastens to introduce* ELAINE, *at whom* MEHTA *is staring.)*

STEPHEN: I see. Well goodness. This Elaine le Fanu from CBS Network.

ELAINE: Very nice to meet you.

MEHTA: My pleasure.

STEPHEN: Stephen Andrews.

MEHTA: And somehow I sense you are a journalist as well.

STEPHEN: I work on a small left-wing magazine.

MEHTA: Yes. I can imagine.

STEPHEN: Mostly it's reviews. And domestic politics. But I'm the youngest, so my brief is the world.

(He smiles. There is a pause.)

You're very hard on journalists in your books.

MEHTA: I?

(He thinks about this a moment, as if it had never occurred to him.)

No.

STEPHEN: *The Vermin Class.* It's not a flattering title for a novel on our profession.

MEHTA: I'm sure Miss le Fanu is not vermin.

(He is looking straight at ELAINE, *the sustained stare of the philanderer.)*

STEPHEN: No.

ELAINE: Have you come far?

MEHTA: I left Heathrow ten hours ago. I left Shropshire—

ELAINE: Ah, your home?

MEHTA: Yes—even earlier.

STEPHEN: You're speaking tomorrow?

MEHTA: Yes. A chore. The necessary prostitution of the intellect. So much is demanded now of the writer which is not writing, which is not the work. The work alone ought to be sufficient. But my publishers plead with me to make myself seen.

STEPHEN: I think you'll find there's great anticipation. I mean, there's some interest as to what you'll say.

(MEHTA *looks away, indifferent.*)

Particularly the comparison with China. It's impossible here not to compare the two cultures . . .

MEHTA: Yes?

STEPHEN: I mean, the way the one, China, is so organized, the other, India, so . . . well, this is a theme you have dealt with in your books.

MEHTA: I suppose.

(*He is still for a moment, lizard-like. Just as* STEPHEN *starts again, he interrupts.*)

STEPHEN: If . . .

MEHTA: Of the Chinese leadership the only one I was able to bring myself to admire wholeheartedly was Chou En-lai.

ELAINE: Ah.

MEHTA: Because he alone among the leaders had the iron self-control not to use his position to publish his own poetry. Chairman Mao, unhappily, not so.

ELAINE: Yes.

(ELAINE *smiles, looks down at the ground, knowingly, having dealt with many such men.*)

Do you not admire Mao?

MEHTA: How can I? Like so many senior statesmen he ruined his credibility by marrying an actress. And what an actress! Madame Mao even claims that she was born beautiful but that in order to identify more closely with the majority of her people, she has managed to will herself ugly. So that even the hideous awfulness of her face is to be marked down as a revolutionary achievement!

(STEPHEN *is frowning.*)

STEPHEN: But there are elements of China . . .

MEHTA: What?

STEPHEN: . . . elements of the Chinese experiment you admire.

MEHTA: I admire nothing in the experiment. I admire China itself.

(As he speaks, WAITERS *enter in rough formation carrying, one by one, a bucket, a bottle, a bag of ice, and glasses.)*
Ah, champagne.

(As he speaks, the glasses are distributed, the bucket set down.)
All old civilizations are superior to younger ones. That is why I have been happiest in Shropshire. They are less subject to crazes. In younger countries there is no culture. The civilization is shallow. Nothing takes root. Even now gangs of crazy youths are sweeping through the streets of Sydney and New York pretending they are homosexual. But do you think they are homosexual really? Of course not. It is the merest fashion. City fashion, that is all. In the old countries, in Paris, in London, when there is a stupid craze, only one person in fifty is affected, but in the young countries there is nothing to hold people back. It is suddenly like the worm factory, everybody fucks everybody, until the next craze, and then everyone will move on and forget and settle down with young women who sell handbags. But meanwhile the damage has been done. The plant has been pulled up at the root and violently plunged back into the earth, so the slow process of growing must begin again. But a worthwhile civilization takes two thousand years to grow.

(The WAITERS *have left.* MEHTA *leans forward to pour himself champagne.)*

STEPHEN: Yes, but . . .

(He gestures at the bottle.) May I? Surely—
(MEHTA has taken one sip and puts his glass aside, where he leaves it, untouched.)

MEHTA: It is not good.

STEPHEN: Surely there's a problem, if what you say is true?

170

(STEPHEN *has got up to pour out a glass for himself and* ELAINE.)
Do you say to those young countries, to so many countries represented in that room, countries with no traditions, no institutions, no civilization as we know it, no old ways of ordering themselves—what do you say? 'Sorry, things will take time . . . it may be bloody in your country at first, but this is an inevitable phase in a young civilization. You must endure dictatorship and bloodshed and barbarity . . .
ELAINE: Mr Mehta wasn't saying that.
STEPHEN: . . . because you are young. There is nothing we can do for you.'
ELAINE: This is . . .
STEPHEN: No, surely not! They must be helped!
MEHTA: Nobody can help.
STEPHEN: What do you mean?
MEHTA: Except by example. By what one is. One is civilized. One is cultured. One is rational. That is how you help other people to live.
(He smiles at ELAINE, *as if only she will understand.* STEPHEN *is staring in disbelief.)*
STEPHEN: You mean you are saying . . . even as someone reaches up to you to be fed . . .
ELAINE: That isn't . . .
MEHTA: If I may . . .
STEPHEN: 'Oh, no I can't fill your bowl . . .
ELAINE: Stephen . . .
STEPHEN: . . . but I would—please—do—like you to admire my civilization: the cut of my suit!'
(MEHTA *is smiling at* ELAINE, *to say he can deal with this.)*
MEHTA: What can you do, he proceeds by parody.
STEPHEN: No.
ELAINE: Stephen's . . .
STEPHEN: No. What you are saying . . .
ELAINE: *(With sudden violence)* Mr Mehta has written about this.

171

(There is a pause. STEPHEN *walks a long way upstage. Pauses. Turns. Walks back down. Picks the bottle out and pours himself another glass. Sits down again. Then* MEHTA *speaks very calmly.)*

MEHTA: It is true that it is hard . . . it is hard to help the poor. Young men like you, who have left the universities, find this sort of talk easy, just as any woman may make a group of men feel guilty with feminist ideas—how easy it is, at dinner tables, to make all the men feel bad, how we do not do our share, how we do not care for their cunts, how their orgasms are not of the right kind, how this, how that, this piece of neglect, this wrong thinking or that—so it is with you, you young men of Europe. You make us all uncomfortable by saying 'The poor! The poor!' But the poor are a convenience only, a prop you use to express your own discontent. Which is with yourself.

(There is a pause.)

(Darkly) I have known many men like you.

*(*ELAINE *is slightly shocked by Mehta's cruelty. But suddenly he seems to relax again.)*

The subject was not the poor. I was not speaking of them. The subject was Australia, and why Barry is suddenly in the bed of Bruce. Do you have views on that?

STEPHEN: No.

MEHTA: No. Because there is no political explanation, so it bores you.

STEPHEN: Did I say?

MEHTA: I know you. I know it from your look.

(He turns away, shaking his head.)

Politics. It is the disease. Narrow politics. That old bastard Marx . . .

STEPHEN: Well . . .

MEHTA: The inflammation of the intellect among the young, the distortion. Every idea crammed through this tiny ideology, everything crammed through the eye of Marxism. Tssh! What nonsense it all is. *(He turns back to* STEPHEN. *Defini-*

172

tively) Socialism, a luxury of the wealthy. To the poor, a suicidal creed.

(Then he gets up, smiling pleasantly, as if the day's work were done.)

Well, I am tired of arguing . . .

STEPHEN: Actually, you haven't argued at all.

MEHTA: What do you mean?

ELAINE: Stephen.

STEPHEN: I don't call what he does arguing at all. You've attributed to me various ideas which you say I hold—on what evidence, I have no idea. Marx you mention. I didn't mention him, or universities, or what I'm supposed to think about the poor. I've said nothing. It was you who dragged it in, just as you dragged in all that peculiar and rather distasteful talk about women's orgasms—something, I must say, I rather gather from your books you have the utmost difficulty in coming to terms with . . .

MEHTA: *(Inflamed)* Ah, now I see!

STEPHEN: Yes!

MEHTA: Underneath all the talk . . .

STEPHEN: Yes!

MEHTA: . . . all the apparent concern for the poor, now we have the true thing, what we really want to say, what he really has to say: he has read my books! And of course he must hurt me.

(STEPHEN *looks down. He answers, still stubborn but also feeble.)*

STEPHEN: I certainly do think they are not very pro-women.

(MEHTA *glowers at him.)*

MEHTA: Ah, well, of course, the ultimate progressive offence among the young men from the universities. In the old days—what was it?—that one must be pro-life; now we must be pro-women . . .

STEPHEN: No.

MEHTA: Well, ask yourself if your heroes are very pro-women, your Lenin, your Castro . . .

173

STEPHEN: He is not *my* Castro.

MEHTA: This ludicrous, long-winded bore who speaks for eight hours on end, who won his battles by speaking whole villages to death—they reeled over, bored in the face of his speeches —this man (we do not say this, it is long forgotten) who was once an extra in an Esther Williams movie.

STEPHEN: There, you're doing it again. I haven't mentioned Castro.

MEHTA: At a conference on poverty, 'Castro! Castro!' It is the chorus of sheep.

STEPHEN: Why do you come? Why do you come here if it's such torture to you?

MEHTA: Yes. And why are you here?

(There is a sudden pause, after the shouting. Sure of his point, MEHTA *now formally turns to* ELAINE.*)*

Miss le Fanu, tonight I am to dine with the Professor of Classical Studies at Delhi University. It is already pre-arranged. He is coming specially, he is flying, as he is keen to hear my views on his new translation of Herodotus.

*(*STEPHEN *speaks quietly as he helps himself, a little drunkenly, to more champagne.)*

STEPHEN: Oh, shit!

MEHTA: *(Ignoring this)* If our conversation would not be tedious to you, I would be delighted if you would join us for dinner, and afterwards perhaps . . .

STEPHEN: He could fuck your arse ragged in an upstairs room.

(An explosion from the others.)

MEHTA: Mr Andrews!

ELAINE: I must say, Stephen . . .

MEHTA: I cannot see how that remark is justified.

*(*STEPHEN *smiles, hovering, drunk, magnificent.)*

STEPHEN: How the right wing always appropriates good manners. Yes? They always have that. Form and decorum. A permanent excuse for not addressing themselves to what people actually say, because they can always turn their heads away if a sentence is not correctly formulated.

A MAP OF THE WORLD

MEHTA: Now it is you who are exaggerating.

STEPHEN: You're like all those people who think that if you say 'Excuse me' at one end of a sentence and 'Thank you' at the other, you are entitled to be as rude as you like in between. English manners!

MEHTA: Whatever one may think of them, it seems, Andrews, it is only the foreigner who bothers with them any more.

STEPHEN: Yes. How appropriate! That you, an Indian by birth, should be left desperately mimicking the manners of a country that died—died in its heart—over thirty, forty, fifty years ago.

(He gestures to the ceiling of the room.)

This sad, pathetic imitation, this room, this conference, these servants,—that all this goes on, like a ghost ship without passengers. The India of the rich! How I despise it!

MEHTA: Yes.

(MEHTA looks at him, watching, not rising to the bait.)

ELAINE: You're smiling.

MEHTA: Yes. It makes me smile suddenly to see the young man . . .

STEPHEN: Stephen.

MEHTA: . . . to see Stephen gesturing. To hear him argue. In Hindi there is no word for 'eavesdropper'. It is not required. Everyone speaks too loud. When I think of my home, it is of men in rooms arguing. And in the streets, the dying. This is India. Without the will to act.

(His sudden characteristic darkness has come over him. Then he turns to ELAINE.)

Miss le Fanu, you are welcome to dine with us.

ELAINE: Thank you.

MEHTA: I have asked your Peggy Whitton.

STEPHEN: Who?

MEHTA: The Peggy Whitton whom I met just now. Do you know her?

STEPHEN: Dark. Attractive.

MEHTA: She is attractive, yes.

STEPHEN: But she said . . .

MEHTA: What?

STEPHEN: That she would dine with me.

(MEHTA moves suddenly and decisively to the door.)

MEHTA: Let her come. Boy!

(The WAITER appears.)

WAITER: Sahib.

MEHTA: Peggy Whitton, who was on the verandah, reading, as I came in. Will you ask her to join us?

(The WAITER goes.)

MEHTA: By chance she was reading one of my books. Then she looked up. The author was before her. She could not believe her good fortune.

(At once PEGGY WHITTON appears. She is in her early twenties, American, in a plain cotton dress. There is a pause.)

PEGGY: Yes?

MEHTA: Miss Whitton. You are over-extended. You appear to be eating in two places at once.

PEGGY: *(Looking between them)* Oh, I see. No. I thought we'd all eat together.

STEPHEN: Mr Mehta is implying this is not on.

MEHTA: I said nothing.

STEPHEN: He dislikes me. Because I don't just listen when he speaks. I dispute. He finds this habit offensive. He is the famous writer. He expects to be allowed to give forth. In his books he makes sure there is no dispute. There are no messy arguments. He writes fiction because in fiction he gets his own way.

(There is a pause.)

Well, have it tonight. Dine with Peggy Whitton. By all means. *(He turns to PEGGY)* Sit at his table. Lie at his feet. Let him pour gold in your ear.

(He goes. PEGGY makes to follow him, upset.)

PEGGY: I must follow the boy. And be nice to him. Excuse me, Mr Mehta.

MEHTA: Of course. Eight o'clock.

PEGGY: Yes.

(There is a pause. She cannot quite leave. MEHTA *is smiling. They are still.)*

PEGGY: I better go.

(At once music begins to play, quietly. She runs off. MEHTA *crosses the room towards us. As he does so, the lights go down, dramatically darkening, until they are in two pools only on* ELAINE *and* MEHTA.)

MEHTA: Why are you smiling?

ELAINE: Oh . . . men I suppose.

MEHTA: Children, you mean. Do you know this Peggy Whitton?

ELAINE: I've met her.

MEHTA: She's a jazz violinist. Reputedly brilliant.

ELAINE: Well, I'm sure you will charm her.

MEHTA: Do you think so?

ELAINE: Yes, of course. If you want her just ask. Do it. Act. Seize her. Never nurse unrequited desire.

*(*ELAINE *gets up from her chair, her acting expanding alarmingly.)*

MEHTA: You say that?

ELAINE: Yes! I've lived by it!

(At once from the darkness, great cries.)

ANGELIS: Lights!

BOOM OPERATOR: Sound!

SOUND RECORDIST: Speed!

ANGELIS: Turn over!

CAMERAMAN: Rolling!

CLAPPERBOY: Mark it! Scene 86. Take 4.

(Huge lights now illuminate ELAINE. *A 35mm camera has circled on to place. Sound men have edged near her.* ELAINE *steps up into her highlight.)*

ANGELIS: Action!

ELAINE: What do you think the purpose of life is? We could be giants. Victor, I swear it's the truth. This mess, this stew of unhappiness. How nobody dares to speak what they feel.

A MAP OF THE WORLD

There's something inside every human being. Something suppressed. It's got to come out. I tell you, Victor; cut through to it. My friend, I beg you: let that something out.

ANGELIS: Cut! All right, yes, print that.

(At once huge lights come on in the studio and the scene fractures. PEGGY WHITTON, *a woman in her early thirties, well dressed in grey cotton trousers and a grey sweater, walks through the chaos. She has been watching the filming of the scene. We are now in* SCENE TWO.)

PEGGY: My God, it's terrible. That wasn't the point of the original scene.

ANGELIS: Please, yes, I am with you in a moment, I am most keen to hear what you say.

STEPHEN: Is Paul there?

ANGELIS: Well done, everyone. Monica, all right?

ELAINE: I don't know. I just don't feel I got her.

ANGELIS: You have her, honestly. That was wonderful. Were you happy, Shashi?

MEHTA: Yes. I was fine.

STEPHEN: Paul!

PAUL: Hi. How are you.

*(*PAUL *is a strikingly good-looking young man, who now embraces the* STEPHEN-*actor. He offers him a small punnet of strawberries.* MAKE-UP GIRL *is dealing with the* ELAINE-*actress's face. The* PROPMEN *are waiting to know whether to take furniture away.)*

MAKE-UP: That was really great.

ELAINE: Thank you, Barbara. There's something happening to this eyelash.

PROPMAN: Do we take these?

SECOND: Are we going back?

CAMERAMAN: Do we need a re-set?

LOADER: Is it the same shot?

ANGELIS: Look, please, everyone, just give me a moment.

(He has raised his voice. There is a silence.)

PEGGY: You've quite destroyed Victor's writing you know.

ANGELIS: Please, everyone, we have a visitor today, who has come to observe our filming. We welcome the real Peggy Whitton, on whom Victor Mehta based his great novel. She made that choice which is at the centre of the book. I am sure she will have all sorts of observations . . . remarks, which will be helpful to us.

(She is looking at him. They are quite still.)

For that reason I think we may need a moment alone.

(A WARDROBE GIRL *walks on, oblivious of the slight tension.)*

WARDROBE GIRL: This hat for Scene Ninety?

ANGELIS: Yes, it's fine.

(Then the MARTINSON-*actor.)*

MARTINSON: Is it me yet?

SCRIPT GIRL: No, your scene's later.

STEPHEN: Angelis, if you need me I'm just stepping out. I'll be in the dressing-room with Paul.

(They go.)

SPARKS: Ten minutes, guv?

ANGELIS: Yes, OK.

FIRST & SPARKS: Ten minutes! Ten minutes everyone!

(Everyone disperses. ANGELIS *calls to the* SCRIPT GIRL.)*

PROPMAN: What can I do with ten minutes?

ANGELIS: By the way, Caroline . . .

SCRIPT GIRL: Yes.

ANGELIS: That hat I was shown. It's ridiculous. Please get it changed.

(The lights have gone down. The studio is almost empty.)

Miss Whitton, be clear. This is not my forte. I am an action director. Cars, fast movement, guns. For motives of tax, my employers are making a more cultural movie. I am told, in order to lose money . . . for reasons it is quite beyond me to understand. Leasebacks, kickbacks, greenbacks, I understand nothing. It was not even meant to be my assignment. Three weeks ago I was about to shoot *Pulveriser 3*. But suddenly instead my business is nuance.

179

PEGGY: I want very little. Only that you should stick to the facts.

ANGELIS: *(He calls off)* Get her a chair. Please. Go on.

PEGGY: For a start, why have you made me a jazz violinist? I was an actress.

ANGELIS: I know. I informed Mr Mehta of the change.

PEGGY: But what's the point of it?

ANGELIS: It adds colour.

PEGGY: Apart from anything, it's just so unlikely. All the jazz violinists you meet in Bombay.

ANGELIS: Does it matter?

PEGGY: Of course. Everything matters. It's a question of tone. For instance, the scene I just saw. The speech 'What do you think the purpose of life is?' Have you heard anyone say anything like that in real life?

ANGELIS: Not in those exact words, no.

PEGGY: What happened happened purely by accident. It was chance. It was chance that I met him. And in a funny way, it was chance what I did.

(There is a pause. ANGELIS looks steadily at her.)

ANGELIS: Perhaps it would be easiest . . . why not tell me the story from your point of view?

(A PROP MAN arrives with a chair. It is set down immediately in front of an unlit brute. The MAN goes. PEGGY sits.)

PEGGY: I was staying in that hotel. I was in Bombay. I was making a film. It was a phoney sort of thriller, a heist movie, maharajahs and diamonds and so on. And I was basically a New York actress. Not even that. I was a philosophy major who worked in publishing. Someone wrote a play and asked me to act. And that's what I did. Easy America. The easiest place in the world.

(She smiles.)

Anyway this movie was dumb. It was long and dumb. I was off for a couple of days. Witty and literate people I was pretty short on, and figured that at least if I went along to this conference I'd read about in the papers . . . well, the great thing would be not to have to talk about films. I had briefly met, I guess for ten minutes maybe, this young Englishman . . . well now, there you are, I looked at the script and in your version you have him as a bore. But that's not how he was. The night I first met him he was . . . charming . . . *(She suddenly gives up the struggle.)* Oh look, this is pointless.

ANGELIS: Please, no, say.

PEGGY: Angelis, you need a decent writer, you know?

ANGELIS: I know.

PEGGY: I can sit here all day and set you right on everything and you still won't be able to show it. That's what writers do. They make you see it. And on this film the screenwriter is terrible. *(She shakes her head.)* Elaine, for instance. I mean she wasn't direct like that. Not Elaine. She always just insinuated. She was always just there. Oh, and she was so warm!

ANGELIS: *(Hurt)* She's warm in this.

PEGGY: She's understanding, yes.

ANGELIS: She's one of the characters the writer's done best.

(PEGGY *looks at him, as if now realizing how deep the gulf is between them. So it is kindly, as to an invalid, that she now speaks.)*

PEGGY: Please, do you think, could you get me a glass of water?

ANGELIS: Yes. I'll get someone . . .

PEGGY: No . . . if you could . . . get it yourself. I need a moment. Just a moment's clarity.

(She smiles, to try and take the offence out of the request.)

PEGGY: If you would give me a moment, then I'll let you get on with your film.

(There's a pause. He turns and goes out. PEGGY *is alone on the set. The brute behind her slowly begins to burn. She speaks straight to us.)*

Young. That's the first thing. Young. Unmistakably young. Not even sure or confident. But irreplaceably, indecently young. You never get it back. How can you? Oh God, nothing makes sense. None of it. Unless you understand this one basic fact. How do I put it? *(She smiles)* That I was so young.

181

A MAP OF THE WORLD

(PEGGY *goes. From the back of the area* VICTOR MEHTA *is appearing, pursued into the conference hall by men in suits. The* CREW *transforms the set by laying out rows of chairs to suggest an empty hall. This is as sketchily marked as the previous Indian scene.* MARTINSON, *a tall Swede, is pursuing* MEHTA.)

MARTINSON: Mr Mehta, please, I must insist. You must not just walk away from me. I am trying to tell you, it is a simple statement. Mr Mehta, you cannot refuse.

(*The lights change. The set is by now assembled.* SCENE THREE *has begun.*)

MEHTA: You ask me to accept it. I cannot accept it. It's out of the question. I am a free writer. The whole subject of my work is freedom. Now you ask me to give my freedom up. Well, I will not.

(MARTINSON *turns despairingly to his colleagues.*)

MEHTA: Peggy! Where is Peggy?

(PEGGY WHITTON *has arrived from the other side.*)

PEGGY: Victor, I'm here.

MEHTA: I am sorry, my dear. I had hoped to have lunch with you. But I am so distressed. There is trouble.

PEGGY: What kind?

MEHTA: Why not ask Mr Martinson? He is running the conference. He is the man who invited me to speak.

(*He gestures at* MARTINSON, *who is standing at the centre of a group of suited diplomats.* MARTINSON *is a tall, grave and persistent Swede, whose apparent doggedness turns out to have an iron quality. He is in his forties.*)

You remember last night . . .

PEGGY: Yes.

MEHTA: . . . after our dinner . . . I told you something here made me uneasy from the start . . .

PEGGY: You enjoyed dinner.

MEHTA: Yes. (*He pauses, thrown by this apparent irrelevance, then persists.*) Yes, I did at the time. But that was last night.

182

And now this morning Mr Martinson has come with this evil news.

MARTINSON: Perhaps, perhaps if I were allowed to repeat it to your friend . . .

MEHTA: Miss Whitton . . .

MARTINSON: It would be a good test. She would be able to judge more dispassionately how serious it is. Miss Whitton? *(A pause.* MEHTA *nods.)*

PEGGY: Okay.

(MARTINSON *turns patiently to* PEGGY.)

MARTINSON: Mr Mehta is upset because there has been an approach from the Mozambique delegation . . .

MEHTA: Mozambique!

MARTINSON: Yes, you said.

MEHTA: There is no such place. It is merely a province of China.

MARTINSON: I am not sure they would necessarily agree.

MEHTA: They are a tongue only. Not even a puppet. They are simply another man's mouth.

(MARTINSON *turns back, apparently almost indifferent.)*

MARTINSON: Well, it is not really central . . .

MEHTA: It is very 'central'.

MARTINSON: *(Ignoring him)* Well, it is not really the point. There is a faction, let us say, from the socialist countries . . .

MEHTA: I . . .

MARTINSON: *(Holding up a hand to silence him)* Yes. From whatever direction . . . that objects to Mr Mehta's presence at the conference. Because of some things he's written about their countries in the past.

(MEHTA, *justified, looks to* PEGGY *for her reaction.)*

MEHTA: You see!

PEGGY: Well, there are some people—

MEHTA: Of course, you are right.

PEGGY: . . . factions that are bound to object to some of Victor's books. I mean, I've only read a couple—sorry, Victor— but what he says doesn't seem to me to read like hostility. He loves the countries; he attacks the regimes. Surely even they can see there's a difference.

MARTINSON: Yes. You're right. But they dislike the implication in some of the novels that anyone who professes Marxist ideas always uses them as a sort of convenience, as if they were justification for whatever terror he wants to commit.

MEHTA: It's true.

MARTINSON: There's a phrase where you call Marxism 'dictatorship's fashionable dress.'

MEHTA: That's a very nice phrase.

MARTINSON: Well, they do find that peculiarly insulting.

PEGGY: Yes. But surely they knew that in advance?

MARTINSON: It still causes great anger.

PEGGY: It can't be overnight they've started to read.

(There is a momentary pause as PEGGY *waits for the explanation.)*

So? What are they suggesting? Are you trying to say he's not allowed to speak?

MARTINSON: No, no, goodness, Miss Whitton . . .

(He turns round and smiles at the DIPLOMATS, *who smile and shake their heads.)*

DIPLOMATS: No! . . .

MARTINSON: No one is suggesting . . . I think that would be terrible. Censorship is something we do not countenance at all.

MEHTA: Oh, really?

MARTINSON: No.

*(*PEGGY *frowns, still not understanding.)*

PEGGY: So?

*(*MARTINSON *has already begun to take a slip of paper from his pocket.)*

MARTINSON: A preliminary statement.

MEHTA: You see!

MARTINSON: That is the suggestion.

PEGGY: What about?

MARTINSON: Well . . .

184

A MAP OF THE WORLD

PEGGY: Is that it there?

MARTINSON: Yes. *(He has unfolded it, white, neat, a single page.)* It's been drafted by a committee, just a short statement, that is all.

PEGGY: Saying what?

MARTINSON: Mr Mehta would read it before going on to give his own talk.

PEGGY: But what does it say?

MARTINSON: It's about the nature of fiction. *(He smiles again, the quiet incendiarist)* I suppose it argues all fiction is lies.

(PEGGY *reacts in disbelief.*)

PEGGY: Oh, my God . . . I don't believe it.

MEHTA: Didn't I say?

MARTINSON: Please.

MEHTA: It is ludicrous.

MARTINSON: No.

(PEGGY *looks at him, lost for a response.*)

PEGGY: How long?

MARTINSON: It's brief. As I say, Mr Mehta would read it out before his address, then he would be free to go on and say whatever he likes.

PEGGY *is about to react, but* MARTINSON *carries on, suddenly on the offensive.)*

Please. I don't like it. I am not easy at suggesting it. It is not the ideal procedure at all. However, bear in mind I am pleading for the survival of my conference. This seems to me a small price to pay.

MEHTA: I don't accept that.

(MARTINSON *looks at him, authoritative.*)

MARTINSON: We are here to discuss world poverty. The conference has taken many years to assemble, and in a week's time, the reluctant governments of the West will return home and try to forget they have ever attended. It is true. Any excuse they can find to dismiss the whole occasion as a shambles they will seize on and exploit. Therefore it is, without question, essential that the conference is given every chance of life,

every chance of success. If Mr Mehta refuses to read out this little concoction, then he will make a fine gesture of individual conscience against the pressures—I will say this and please do not repeat it—of less than scrupulous groups, and he will go home to Shropshire, and he will feel proud and clever and generally excellent. And *Time* magazine will write of him, yes, and there will be editorials on the bloody writer's freedom, hurrah! But the conference will be destroyed. It is a short statement, it is an unimportant statement, because it is on a subject which is of no conceivable general interest or importance, namely, what a novel is, which I can hardly see is a subject of vital and continuing fascination to the poor. Frankly, who cares? is my attitude, and I think you will find it is the attitude of all the non-aligned countries . . .
(He looks behind him for confirmation, and the DIPLOMATS *all nod.)*
Certainly, the Scandinavian bloc . . .

DIPLOMATS: Yes . . . Indeed, it is our attitude.

MARTINSON: What is your phrase? We do not give a toss what a novel is. I think I may even say this is Scandinavia's official position, and if a man stands up at the beginning of this afternoon's session and lies about what a novel is, I will just be grateful because then there is a better chance that aid will flow, because grain will flow, because water will flow . . .

MEHTA: This is blackmail!

MARTINSON: No.

MEHTA: Exploitation of our feelings of guilt! In the West we are always being asked to feel guilty. And so we must pay a price in lies!

PEGGY: The West?

MEHTA: Drag us down to their standards!
(He has got up and is now standing in animated argument with himself.)
No, it is wrong!
(MARTINSON *turns coolly to* PEGGY.)

MARTINSON: Miss Whitton?

186

(She as been sitting quietly through Martinson's explanation.)

PEGGY: *(Very casually)* Well, I mean, we should hear it, shouldn't we?

MEHTA: What?

PEGGY: The statement.

(PEGGY *turns to* MEHTA.)

Have you read it?

MEHTA: Are you mad? I did not write it, therefore I shall not read it.

PEGGY: *(To* MARTINSON) Read it.

MEHTA: Don't.

(Then, before MEHTA *can interrupt:)*

PEGGY: Victor. Last night, when we went upstairs—to the bedroom.

MEHTA: Yes, all right, thank you . . .

(She then turns and flashes a smile at MARTINSON.)

PEGGY: We only met last night.

(MEHTA *looks at her beadily. Then, with bitter quiet:)*

MEHTA: All right. Very well, yes, let us hear it. Thank you, Peggy.

(He sits down to listen. PEGGY *smiles.* MARTINSON *begins very formally.)*

MARTINSON: 'Fiction, by its very nature, must always be different from fact, so in a way a man who stands before you as a writer of fiction is already half-way towards admitting that a great deal of what he makes up and invents is as much with an eye to entertainment . . . as it is to presenting literal historical truth . . .

(MEHTA *gets up, exploding.)*

MEHTA: No, no, no, no! It is not to be endured.

PEGGY: Victor . . .

MEHTA: It is Nazi.

PEGGY: It is not Nazi.

MEHTA: It is Nazi.

187

(For the first time PEGGY *starts taking enthusiastic part in the argument, enjoying herself.)*

PEGGY: 'Nazi' means 'National Socialist'. This is not National Socialist. It is not German propaganda of the thirties.

MEHTA: It is neo-Nazi.

PEGGY: No, it is a serious proposition.

MEHTA: Nonsense.

PEGGY: . . . to which we may listen rationally and calmly and as adults, and say, 'Yes, mmm, this is so, this is not so.' Let us therefore . . .

MEHTA: The woman is driving me crazy.

PEGGY: . . . exercise our minds and address the real, the central problem of the day, which is: is all fiction distortion? Come on, let's examine this. I did a term paper. What do we mean by distortion? Are these good arguments on this piece of paper or are they bad?

MEHTA: Not enough the moral blackmail of the Third World, but now we have sexual blackmail. A poor man who stumbles into a bed . . . *(He turns to explain to* MARTINSON.) I have slept with this woman last night; this woman I have embraced . . .

PEGGY: *(Delighted, pretending shock)* Really Victor, you mustn't disclose to the entire UNESCO Secretariat . . .

MEHTA: I approach this woman, a dinner with friends, a conversation about Greek history, an understanding as between strangers that they will spend a night . . . a civilized arrangement . . .

PEGGY: *(Smiles)* Yes.

MEHTA: . . . and now she must betray me.

(PEGGY *smiles at him warmly, her mischievousness past.)*

PEGGY: Nobody betrays you, Victor. Perhaps Martinson is right. That in the scale of things this doesn't matter very much.

(There is a pause as MEHTA *stands alone, touched. Then he nods.)*

188

MEHTA: Bring me the man who has written this. I will negotiate.

(At the back one of the DIPLOMATS *goes out.)*

I do this because she is beautiful. No other reason, yes? Why did Victor Mehta read the statement on the nature of fiction at the UNESCO conference in Bombay in 1978? For thighs, and hair that falls across the face.

(At once STEPHEN ANDREWS *comes in, smiling, talking to the* DIPLOMAT. *He is followed by* M'BENGUE, *a Senegalese in his thirties, small, bright, elegant.* STEPHEN *is gracious, but pleased.)*

STEPHEN: Ah, well, this is excellent!

PEGGY: Stephen!

STEPHEN: I hear there is to be a climb-down. Thank goodness. The whole conference is endangered, I heard . . .

MEHTA: What? Is it him?

STEPHEN: For something so petty, so meaningless . . .

MEHTA: *(Quietly)* Peggy . . .

PEGGY: I didn't know.

STEPHEN: This is my friend M'Bengue of Senegal. He helped us draft . . .

MEHTA: Then I will not read it. No, if it is Mr Andrews . . .

(He turns away. STEPHEN *smiles.)*

STEPHEN: . . . these few remarks.

(Between them MARTINSON *looks puzzled.)*

MARTINSON: Are you old enemies?

MEHTA: No. He insulted me on my arrival here last night, and now I see, yes, it is because of Peggy, because he was to dine with her. That is the motive behind this fine display of principle. She stood him up to dine with me.

PEGGY: *(Looks down)* Oh, lord.

*(*MARTINSON *is still frowning.)*

MARTINSON: Well, this does not mean . . . surely the person must be separate from the argument?

MEHTA: No, absolutely not.

MARTINSON: The motive for the argument does not affect its

validity. As Miss Whitton said, a thing is true or untrue, worth proposing or not worth proposing . . .

MEHTA: No!

MARTINSON: . . . no matter who proposes it. As for instance as one might say of Hitler's love of Wagner . . .

PEGGY: *(Groaning)* Oh, my God . . .

MARTINSON: . . . it does not mean . . .

MEHTA: Let us not . . .

MARTINSON: . . . that Wagner's music is discredited . . .
(The DIPLOMATS *shake their heads in agreement.)*

DIPLOMATS: No.

PEGGY: Please.

MARTINSON: And so it is for whatever . . . I cannot say this well . . .

MEHTA: Indeed.

MARTINSON: . . . reason it is that he comes . . .

MEHTA: *(Exasperated at* MARTINSON's *dogged logic)* But you said, you yourself said, less than scrupulous groups were using this argument to threaten . . .

MARTINSON: But you, Mr Mehta, your motives. Only a moment ago you were saying it was not for principle that you would speak; it was for thighs.

M'BENGUE: *(To* STEPHEN) Thighs?

MEHTA: I would give in, yes. Then. But now I will not give in. I am shaken awake.
*(*ELAINE *comes in, very cheerful.)*

ELAINE: Hey, I hear this is getting very interesting.

MARTINSON: I'm not sure.

MEHTA: *(At once)* Please, no, nothing now, not in front of the press . . .

ELAINE: Off the record?
*(*MARTINSON *looks across to* MEHTA, *who nods.* MARTINSON *takes advantage of the moment to reassert his chairmanship.)*

MARTINSON: All right. Let us please to put motive aside. Let us examine the true reason for the dispute. You agree?
*(*MEHTA *looks at him without enthusiasm, but he goes on.)*

Let us try to understand the feelings of the African countries in particular. Well, M. M'Bengue can explain.

(There is a pause. The others look to M'BENGUE.*)*

M'BENGUE: It is true that we have chosen you, Mr Mehta, and it is to a degree arbitrary. There is a greater argument and we are using you as an instrument merely to draw attention to it. It happens that your novels are full of the most provocative observations—I will not linger on them. In particular, what you say of Madame Mao . . .

MARTINSON: *(Panicking)* Oh no.

MEHTA: *(With renewed vigour)* Ah well, yes.

M'BENGUE: You lack respect . . .

MEHTA: You ask me to desist from writing of Madame Mao?

M'BENGUE: No.

MEHTA: No, I cannot. I am a comic novelist. It would be super-human to refrain . . .

MARTINSON: It is not the point.

MEHTA: You ask me to refrain from writing of a woman who does not dare to make public the date of her birthday because she is afraid it will over-excite the masses?

(He stares insanely at M'BENGUE.*)*

She is a gift. You ask me not to write of her.

MARTINSON: *(Quietly leading* M'BENGUE *back)* The greater argument, M. M'Bengue, please.

STEPHEN: Go on.

M'BENGUE: Very well, it is this. We take aid from the West because we are poor, and in everything we are made to feel our inferiority. The price you ask us to pay is not money but misrepresentation. The way the nations of the West make us pay is by representing us continually in their organs of publicity as bunglers and murderers and fools. I have spent time in England and there the yellow press does not speak of Africa except to report how a nun has been raped, or there has been a tribal massacre, or how we are slaughtering the elephants— the elephants who are so much more suitable for television programmes than the Africans—or how corrupt and incompetent such-and-such a government is. If the crop succeeds, it is not news. If we build a dam, it is called boring. 'Oh, we do not report the building of dams,' say your newspapers. Dam-building is dull. Boring. The white man's word for everything with which he does not wish to come to terms. Yes, he will give us money, but the price we will pay is that he will not seek to understand our point of view. Pro-Moscow, pro-Washington, that is the only way you can see the world. All your terms are political, and your politics is the crude fight between your two great blocs. Is Angola pro-Russian? Is it pro-American? These are the only questions you ever ask yourselves. As if the whole world could be seen in those terms. In your terms. In the white man's terms and through the white man's media.

(He looks down, as if to hide the strength of feeling behind what he says.)

And so it hurts . . . it begins to hurt that the context of the struggle in Africa is never made clear. It is never explained. Your news agencies report our events, and from a point of view which is eccentric and sensational. All this, day in, day out, we endure and make no protest, and when we come to take part in this conference in Bombay, we find that UNESCO has invited a particular keynote speaker—a black man himself, though of course, because he is Indian, it is not how he sees himself: he thinks himself superior to the black man from the bush—a speaker whose reputation is for wit at the expense of others, whose reporting is not positive, so of course he is called a hero in the West. He is called a bringer of truths because he seeks to discredit those who struggle. And so it is true, yes, in the middle of the night, Mr Andrews and I, walking to the Gateway of India, did say: the greater, the larger misrepresentation we can do nothing about—those who control the money will control the information—but the lesser one, yes, and tonight. A stand is possible.

(He turns to MEHTA.*)* You distort things in your novels because it is funny to distort, because indeed the surface of things is

192

funny, if you do not understand how that surface comes to be, if you do not look underneath. Just as a funeral may be funny to a small boy who sees it passing in the street and does not know the man who is dead. So also no doubt in Africa it is superficially funny to see us blundering about. But who makes the jokes? The rich nations.

MEHTA: No.

M'BENGUE: Jokes, Mr Mehta, are a product of security. If one is secure, one may laugh at others. That is the truth. Humour, like everything, is something you buy. Free speech? Buy. But what is this freedom? The luxury of the rich who are sure of what they have.

(MEHTA *just looks at him.*)

MEHTA: *(Quietly)* What would you do? Ban it?

M'BENGUE: No. I would ask that black men who ascend from their countries do not conspire in the humiliation of those they have left behind.

(There is a pause. When MEHTA *replies it is with a gravity that matches* M'BENGUE*'s.)*

MEHTA: People are venal and stupid and corrupt, no more so now than at any other time in history. They tell themselves lies. The writer asks no more than the right to point those lies out. What you say of how the press sees you is probably true, and the greater grievance you have I am sure is right. But I will not add to the lies.

(There is a pause. And then he gets up.)

And that is all I have to say.

PEGGY: Victor . . .

MEHTA: No.

(MEHTA *goes out. The whole group is suspended for a moment, and* M'BENGUE *gets up and leaves at the other side.* MARTINSON *looks behind him to one of his* AIDES.)

MARTINSON: The educational motion from tomorrow's agenda . . .

AIDE: Yes.

MARTINSON: We may move it to today?

193

AIDE: It's possible.

MARTINSON: Delay Mr Mehta's address until tomorrow. If that's agreeable?

(He looks to STEPHEN.)

STEPHEN: Yes.

MARTINSON: The Committee, Mr Andrews, will give us twenty-four hours?

STEPHEN: *(Conscious of* PEGGY'S *gaze)* Of course.

(MARTINSON *gets up and leads his team out silently.* ELAINE, PEGGY *and* STEPHEN *are left alone.)*

STEPHEN: Well, there you are.

ELAINE: I'd thought M'Bengue was a fool . . .

STEPHEN: No.

ELAINE: When we watched him yesterday, he seemed to be the worst kind of professional politician.

STEPHEN: How wrong can you be? Don't you think? Don't you think, Peggy?

PEGGY: Oh, yes. He's got a good case.

(She is thoughtful. She starts to move.)

STEPHEN: Are you off?

PEGGY: Why?

STEPHEN: I was wondering, no, I'm sorry, it was silly. I wanted to have lunch. Fuck, I shouldn't have mentioned it. Forget I mentioned it.

ELAINE: Why doesn't everyone just eat their meals on a tray in their room?

PEGGY: I just don't believe it. Why do people make things so hard? Stephen, last night if you were so upset about dinner, why didn't you say?

STEPHEN: Only slightly. And that's not the whole story.

PEGGY: I ran down the corridor, I tried to find you after you made that ridiculous scene.

STEPHEN: I'd gone.

PEGGY: I know.

STEPHEN: I was sickened by Mehta.

PEGGY: It's so *typical.* If you'd stayed we could have discussed

194

it. But no—throw the whole chess table over. Now we have a problem. Well?

STEPHEN: Well what?

PEGGY: Well, we've got to get them to sit down and talk.

STEPHEN: Do you mean M'Bengue and Victor?

PEGGY: Of course.

STEPHEN: Why us?

ELAINE: Not me, I'm press.

STEPHEN: Anyway, it's hardly likely.

PEGGY: Why not?

STEPHEN: Well I know this will seem a very minor objection. But they do actually believe different things.

PEGGY: So what would you do?

STEPHEN: Do?

PEGGY: Yes, do.

STEPHEN: *(Shrugs)* Do nothing. Either Victor agrees his novels are slanted and malicious—which they are—or we can kiss goodbye to the conference.

PEGGY: And what? What then, Stephen? You would like to go off and *have lunch?*

STEPHEN: *(Stung)* No.

(PEGGY *suddenly smiles.*)

PEGGY: Oh God, Stephen, I do understand you. In Westchester County I knew lots of people like you.

STEPHEN: Thank you.

PEGGY: You know, life can really be quite easy, if you don't always let your emotions get in the way.

(He looks at her a moment.)

When I was sixteen, I made a resolution. I had a girlfriend, we were walking in the Rockies, and the view, I can tell you, was something as we came over to Boulder, Colorado. And we had a six-pack right there on top of the mountain. And she was a good girl. I mean a really good girl. You could trust your life to her. And there that day we looked over the valley. We thought about our lives and relationships, and said, 'Life can be simple, by will we can make it simple. From now on we are

195

totally free. Let's not ever mess with the bad things at all.'
Now what's sad is I saw her six months ago. She's married to a
lawyer in DC and he's never there, he's out over-achieving all
day, she doesn't like him when he is there, and so she's fucking around, so that one day, she told me, she got this terrible
pain here. She was really desperate. Into the hospital. She
told me for the first time in her life she prayed. And I said
'Really, what was your prayer, Elise?' And she said 'Oh God,
let it not be cervical cancer. God please. God, just do this for
me. If it's not cancer, I swear I'll never cheat on Arnold again.
And that . . . *(She laughs delightedly.)* . . . I tell you that,
when I come to write my novel about America, that will be its
title: *Cheating on Arnold.* That will be its name. Because you
see that is not what is going to happen to me. You understand?
Because there is no need.
*(She says this with the complete conviction of youth. Then
smiles.)*
Now the two of you, Victor, you, both slightly ridiculous,
slightly contemptible, in my view, you see? Elaine will agree.
That sort of behaviour, men being jealous, men fighting, it's
out of date. Outdated, Stephen. Unnecessary, Stephen. I
mean, drop the bad behaviour and you might get somewhere.

STEPHEN: Meaning I will get somewhere?

PEGGY: Drop the bad behaviour and you will get somewhere.
(A silence while this sinks in. ELAINE *looks down, amused.*
STEPHEN *cautious, but enjoying his power.)*

STEPHEN: That's kind of you, but the fact is, I didn't act alone.

PEGGY: Ah, well.

STEPHEN: There's a committee.

PEGGY: *(Vigorously)* Well, I'm not offering all of them.
(ELAINE smiles.)
Even Westchester County has its limits, you know.

STEPHEN: Yes, but I just helped draft the statement, there are
others and they do have views.

PEGGY: They can be swung.

STEPHEN: Because they're black?

(PEGGY *looks at him with contempt.*)

PEGGY: That's when you're really boring, Stephen. The sex drops off you. It's like your prick drops off when you say things like that.

STEPHEN: All right.

PEGGY: No, not because they're black, you wimp, but because it's a committee of—how many?

STEPHEN: Six.

PEGGY: Right. And you're on it, that's all. And when you're not apologizing for your own existence, you can actually be quite a plausible human being.

(STEPHEN *looks at her, touched.*)

STEPHEN: Weren't you moved by what M'Bengue said just now?

PEGGY: Stephen, whose cause does he damage by stopping the conference?

STEPHEN: He doesn't want to stop the conference.

PEGGY: His own.

STEPHEN: But . . .

PEGGY: Senegal's. Somalia's. Mozambique's.

STEPHEN: But if Victor could be persuaded.

PEGGY: Victor was persuaded. I had him persuaded. Until you appeared.

(There's a pause. Then PEGGY *turns, as if finally despairing.)*
All right, then, make your little stand . . .

STEPHEN: It's not that.

PEGGY: . . . whatever it is. No one will remember.

STEPHEN: It's principle.

PEGGY: Principle, indeed! People do what they want to, then afterwards, if it suits them, they call it principle.

STEPHEN: No.

PEGGY: Rationalization of what you've already decided, that's what principle is.

(STEPHEN *is already shaking his head.*)

STEPHEN: Certain things are important. Certain things are good.

A MAP OF THE WORLD

PEGGY: How can you say, you who are not involved? M'Bengue, sure, he's a member of a government . . .

STEPHEN: He's a civil servant.

PEGGY: All right, he's a civil servant who represents a government which stands to gain from the successful outcome of this conference—so when he says 'principle,' we listen. It's at some cost. It's at some personal expense. But your principles come from a store on the corner and cost you nothing.

(STEPHEN *looks down, very hurt.*)

STEPHEN: No, well, I'm sorry . . .

PEGGY: Look, Stephen, I don't mean to be unkind to you. I like you.

ELAINE: *(Smiles)* She does.

PEGGY: You attract unkindness because so often you're not you. You're this ragbag of opinions.

STEPHEN: So are you.

(PEGGY *looks at him, surprised, not understanding.*)

How is it different? Your freedom you've just told us about, your sexual freedom, what's that if not some contrived and idiotic idea based on some mountaintop experience you've talked yourself into believing was a revelation? And a revelation meaning what? That you may sleep with anyone and not get involved. Gosh, well, thank goodness. What a convenient discovery. Remind me to buy climbing boots next time I'm out.

ELAINE: Stephen . . .

STEPHEN: The six-pack philosopher. Really! Entitled to patronize. To witter on about freedom. And from what position? From the safety of beauty. From the absolute safety of being beautiful.

(*He stops, aware of having hurt her. He begins to apologize.*)

Well, I'm sorry. Something happened to me last night, while you were no doubt with . . .

PEGGY: Victor.

STEPHEN: Quite. I walked to the Gateway of India with M'Bengue, among the small kerosene stoves, suffocating, the

198

heat, the dope, tripping against beggars, watching boys of ten and eleven with fat joints stuck in their mouths. We walked along Chowpatty Beach, and I listened to a man trying to explain to me what it's like to see the world the other way up. To come—can you imagine—from Dakar, West Africa, to fly through the night and arrive in this conference hall to listen to the well-heeled agents of the West argue that of course aid never gets through, and, when it gets through, how officials rip it off. And how really all it does is create a disease called aid dependency. Aid doesn't really help, the West keeps saying to salve its bloated conscience. Yes, I do feel these things that seem to you affectations only because to believe in anything now in the West, except money or sex or motor cars, is to mark yourself out as foolish. A subject for satire. At which Victor Mehta is adept.

(There is a pause. PEGGY *looks at him, lost. Then suddenly:)*

PEGGY: Then you should argue it out.

STEPHEN: What?

PEGGY: The two of you. Just the two of you on behalf of your committee. Since you believe it so strongly.

STEPHEN: He won't listen.

ELAINE: He'll listen. If Peggy says . . .

(There is a pause.)

STEPHEN: I'm not sure.

PEGGY: Yes. This evening.

ELAINE: I will adjudicate.

PEGGY: Brilliant! Elaine will decide. And whoever wins, wins me.

STEPHEN: No!

PEGGY: Oh yes. Yes. That will be principle. That's what principle is. Having something to lose.

STEPHEN: No.

PEGGY: That's freedom. I do actually believe in it.

STEPHEN: That's not freedom. My God. That's bartering.

PEGGY: Elaine?

STEPHEN: It's sick.

ELAINE: Putting her body where her mouth is, how can that be wrong?

STEPHEN: It's impossible. What would I say to M'Bengue and the others, if I lost, 'Oh, I'm sorry, because of a deal I made we now have to give way to this offensive Indian . . .' No, it's ridiculous!

PEGGY: Yes, if you lose. But you told me you believed so passionately . . . if you're right after all, if Victor is wrong to say all these things . . .

STEPHEN: He is.

PEGGY: Very well then. Test it. Test it, Stephen. If you want me, argue it tonight.

(She goes out. ELAINE *and* STEPHEN *are left alone.)*

STEPHEN: Oh, God. Elaine . . .

(ELAINE *looks at him affectionately.)*

ELAINE: There's so much passion in you, so much emotion, all the time. This is wrong, that's wrong. Well, tonight you will get the chance to direct that emotion, and in a good cause. *(A pause.)*

What better cause than Peggy Whitton, eh?

(There is a moment of warmth between them. Suddenly they both smile at the ludicrousness of the situation.)

Come on, I'll buy you lunch.

(And at once, ANGELIS *appears from the back of the stage, walking on to the set and calling to his unseen followers. This time the two scenes interweave, one group of people walking right through the other.* SCENE THREE *oblivious to* SCENE FOUR's *existence.)*

ANGELIS: Lunch, everyone.

(ELAINE *and* STEPHEN *are still standing looking at each other.)*

ELAINE: I'm fond of you. You're a fool, and I'm fond of you.

ANGELIS: Strike the set!

ELAINE: Where shall we eat?

STEPHEN: I want to go to the Temple of the Jains. Have you been there?

200

ELAINE: No.

STEPHEN: I hear it's beautiful.

(The PROP CREW *has appeared and is clearing away the chairs.* ELAINE *and* STEPHEN *walk upstage.)*

ELAINE: And let's go to Doongarwadi, to the Parsee funeral ground.

STEPHEN: Is that where the vultures pick at the bodies of the dead?

ELAINE: That's the one.

STEPHEN: Good. Let's go there.

(The lights lose them as they go.)

Lunch before?

ELAINE: After, I think.

(The ASSISTANT *has carried on a chair for* ANGELIS's *approval.)*

ASSISTANT: Is this the right kind of chair for the bedroom, Mr Angelis?

ANGELIS: Yes, that's fine.

ASSISTANT: They want you to look at the bed.

ANGELIS: I will look at the bed later. The bed comes later.

(A CREWMAN *walks by with a ghetto-blaster playing Barry Manilow's 'I am Music'.)*

ASSISTANT: They want to know whether to make the bed soft or hard?

ANGELIS: Soft.

ASSISTANT: What colour?

ANGELIS: Blue. Blue spread.

ASSISTANT: Really?

ANGELIS: *(Panicking now)* White. Oh, God. I don't know. White sheets, white spread too. Sure. What the hell? Who cares? Get the book.

ASSISTANT: The book says white.

ANGELIS: Then white. If it's in the book, it must be right.

(The set has been cleared. There is only an empty floor. PEGGY WHITTON *runs on, as if the set were still there. She doesn't realize* STEPHEN *and* ELAINE *have gone.)*

A MAP OF THE WORLD

PEGGY: Stephen! Victor agrees. It's on.
(She stands triumphant. ANGELIS *does not see or hear her.)*
ANGELIS: I'm bored.
(A great cry.)
Lunch! Lunch!

ACT TWO

At the end of the interval, in the darkness, we hear a recording of Peggy's letter home.

PEGGY: Dear Sue, Alone but not lonely in Bombay. I have met a man—I cannot tell you—I have met a novelist, Victor Mehta. A man of great gracefulness. Difficult, of course, like the best men. And very proud. In a fit of stupidity, I have agreed—oh, God, how I agreed to this I have no idea—I have agreed to sleep with the winner of an argument. One of the men is Victor. The other . . . not.

SCENE FIVE. *The film studio. There is now a bedroom, which is represented by a bed and a wall behind with a door in it, which leads off to an imaginary bathroom. The room is unnaturally spacious, occupying a large area, detailed but incomplete. Dotted near it are canvas chairs and camera equipment, though the camera itself is missing. The actors are sitting about in casual clothes, waiting for rehearsal. They are not yet in costume. The* ELAINE-*actress is sitting at one side by herself with a magazine. The* MARTINSON-*actor is doing* The Times *crossword. He was born an Englishman, but is now a self-consciously international figure in blue jeans, gold medallion and muted Californian T-shirt. The* M'BENGUE-*actor stands in the middle, quite still, looking off into the distance.*

M'BENGUE: Well, what is happening?

MARTINSON: I don't know. *(He frowns.)* What on earth could be one . . . two . . . three . . . four . . . five . . . six . . . seven letters, begins with Z, and the clue is 'It's the plague of the earth'?

203

A MAP OF THE WORLD

ELAINE: Zionism.

MARTINSON: What?

(The PEGGY-actress comes on. She is wearing a band round her head, to push her hair back. She has a dressing-gown on over her shirt and trousers.)

PEGGY: Is there any sign of Angelis?

ELAINE: No. We're all called, but there's nobody here.

(MARTINSON is staring at ELAINE in disbelief.)

MARTINSON: What d'you mean, 'Zionism'?

ELAINE: Well, it's seven letters, beginning with Z.

MARTINSON: But are you just saying it because it's a word?

ELAINE: It's a word.

MARTINSON: I know it's a word.

(He pauses.)

I know it's a word.

ELAINE: It's got seven letters and it begins with Z.

(PEGGY has stood a moment, taking no notice, and now smiles round.)

PEGGY: I want to show you a few bathrobes, and then you can say what's best for the scene, OK?

(She disappears through the door in the set and closes it. From the side the STEPHEN-actor appears, in loose grey flannels and pullover, with a book. He is a pleasant and easy-going man. He sits.)

STEPHEN: Hello.

MARTINSON: But are you also saying it's the plague of the earth?

ELAINE: What?

MARTINSON: Zionism.

ELAINE: *(Frowns)* Well, I don't think it's a very good thing, if that's what you mean.

(She goes back to reading, but MARTINSON looks round to see who else is taking notice, then persists.)

MARTINSON: No, that's not actually what I mean. What I mean is, are you actually suggesting that Zionism is the plague of the earth?

ELAINE: Well, obviously, if it's got seven letters and begins with

A MAP OF THE WORLD

Z, it scarcely matters what I think about it. What matters is
what the compiler thinks, and obviously, I don't know, perhaps *The Times* has Arab crossword compilers these days.
Perhaps they have some Libyan on the staff.

MARTINSON: I suppose you think that's funny.

ELAINE: No, I don't think it's funny. I'm just saying . . .

(PEGGY *has come through the bathroom door in a blue-and-
white spotted dressing-gown.*)

PEGGY: Well, what d'you think?

MARTINSON: Very nice.

PEGGY: Monica?

ELAINE: Fine.

STEPHEN: *(Looking up)* Honestly, it's fine.

(PEGGY *goes out smiling.* MARTINSON *is still waiting.*)

MARTINSON: Are you seriously saying . . .

ELAINE: I'm not saying anything.

MARTINSON: . . . you actually think *The Times* would employ
somebody. . . ?

ELAINE: No.

MARTINSON: Do you know the history of the state of Palestine?

ELAINE: Well, as a matter of fact, yes, I do.

MARTINSON: Do you know what happened to the Jews between 1939 and 1945?

ELAINE: Yes, I do. They got wiped out.

MARTINSON: It's not funny.

ELAINE: I know it's not funny, for Christ's sake. I am not for one
second saying it is funny. It's you that seems determined to
take issue with everything I say.

MARTINSON: I'm not.

ELAINE: It's just . . . objectively . . . it seems a remarkable
fact that a people who once enjoyed the sympathy of the
whole world for what they had suffered have, in the space of
just thirty-five years, managed to squander that sympathy by
creating a vicious, narrow-minded, militaristic state.

MARTINSON: *(Quietly)* What?

205

ELAINE: And as a matter of fact, I think it not funny at all. I think it a tragedy.

(There is a pause. Then MARTINSON *turns to appeal to the others.)*

MARTINSON: Did you hear what she just said?

M'BENGUE: *(Neutrally)* Yes, I did.

MARTINSON: *(Turning back to* ELAINE) Do you know what Sartre said?

ELAINE: Yes, I do.

(There is a pause.)

What did he say?

MARTINSON: Why say you did?

ELAINE: Well, I mean, I know what Sartre said about various things . . .

MARTINSON: Such as?

ELAINE: Well, I mean, I can't remember what things he said what about . . . I mean . . . I know he liked actresses very much . . .

(MARTINSON *ignores this.)*

MARTINSON: I will tell you what he said about Israel. That it was a historical exception.

(PEGGY *reappears, in a yellow dressing-gown this time.)*

PEGGY: Guys, this one?

MARTINSON: Very nice.

ELAINE: Sure.

(PEGGY *goes out again.)*

MARTINSON: That normally the Jews would have no right to the territory of Palestine, but that the crime against them was so great, that it was so out of proportion with anything any people had ever suffered before, that it was necessary to make a historical exception and say, 'Yes, give them the land.'

(A pause. ELAINE *concedes with ill grace.)*

ELAINE: OK.

MARTINSON: That's what Sartre said.

ELAINE: OK.

206

A MAP OF THE WORLD

(M'BENGUE *has leant over casually and is looking down at* MARTINSON's *discarded* Times.)

M'BENGUE: It's not Z anyway.

MARTINSON: What?

M'BENGUE: Look, six down is 'evasion'. You don't spell that with a Z. You spell it with an S.

MARTINSON: Are you telling me how to do this?

M'BENGUE: Which means fourteen across is now a seven-letter word beginning with S.

(MARTINSON *looks at him unkindly.*)

MARTINSON: I suppose you agree with her.

M'BENGUE: What?

MARTINSON: About the Jews.

(ELAINE *gets up from her chair, suddenly losing her temper.*)

ELAINE: For Christ's sake, man . . .

(PEGGY *has reappeared in stripes.*)

PEGGY: What do you think?

ELAINE: *(Shouts)* It sucks.

(She throws up her hands in the air, apologizing.) No, I'm sorry. It's just . . . What are we doing? Where is Angelis?

PEGGY: I want to do the scene.

(Everyone momentarily lost, before STEPHEN *looks up again, mild, oblivious.)*

STEPHEN: Why are policemen so important in homosexual mythology?

M'BENGUE: Pardon?

STEPHEN: It's . . . I'm reading about E. M. Forster. What everyone admires in him is not . . . you know . . . books, I mean that's what he wrote, but what everyone really admires him for was having a boyfriend who was a policeman.

M'BENGUE: Well, it is an achievement.

STEPHEN: I suppose. *(He smiles to himself.)* P. C. Bob Buckingham.

(MARTINSON *is frowning, ready to hold forth again.*)

MARTINSON: But in a sense it's absolutely symbolic in a way, isn't it?

207

ELAINE: *(Quietly)* Oh, God.

MARTINSON: Surely what he was doing was forcing the authoritarian figure, in a sense, to yield . . . I'm just talking out loud here . . .

(ELAINE looks across at PEGGY, close to murder. Then goes and lies down on the bed in the fake room.)

In some way the father-figure perhaps . . .

ELAINE: Oh, Jesus, where is Angelis?

MARTINSON: He was seducing him and in some way he was forcing him to admit that his authority was an act, that underneath the social role we all play, we are all . . .

STEPHEN: What?

MARTINSON: Well, you know . . .

STEPHEN: What?

(MARTINSON pauses.)

MARTINSON: Gay.

(STEPHEN frowns, mystified. MARTINSON hastens to qualify.)

I mean, not exclusively. We're not, exclusively. Obviously, you would know more about this. If you've seen those films about fish, it's clear. It's been proved biologically. Sometimes it's one thing, sometimes the other . . .

ELAINE: *(Calling from the bed)* And sometimes fuck-all if they're anything like the rest of us.

(MARTINSON explodes.)

MARTINSON: Will somebody please tell this woman . . .

STEPHEN: It's all right, honestly. She's just provoking you.

(STEPHEN smiles, placating. MARTINSON goes on, the air tense.)

MARTINSON: We pay a price for suppressing this truth. That we are all bisexual. We hide this fact at enormous expense to ourselves in order to obey some imaginary social norm. But the result of this suppression is great damage inside. Finally . . . yes . . . we implode.

STEPHEN: Yes, well . . .

MARTINSON: Literally!

STEPHEN: *(Puzzled)* It's a problem.

MARTINSON: Yes.

(At once ANGELIS *sweeps on, followed by* ASSISTANTS.)

ANGELIS: I am sorry, my friends . . .

PEGGY: Angelis!

ANGELIS: . . . I have been delayed. Crew!

(All the actors get up as he calls out.)

ELAINE: Thank God. We were all about to implode.

ANGELIS: Please, we move on, we prepare the scene.

(PEGGY *moves on to the set as* ELAINE *and* MARTINSON *leave it.* STEPHEN *quiet, near* ANGELIS.)

STEPHEN: Has there been trouble?

ANGELIS: No. No trouble.

STEPHEN: I thought perhaps . . .

ANGELIS: What?

(The furniture in the room is changed round by the CREW, *setting it right.)*

STEPHEN: We had heard that Mehta was coming.

ANGELIS: Mehta is coming, yes.

(He moves away, passing ELAINE *who has collected her script.)*

Monica, all well?

ELAINE: Fine, thank you.

(ANGELIS *turns, looking at the set.)*

ANGELIS: Please, now, everyone, we rehearse. It is what? It is the evening. The scene is evening. Peggy at last begins to have her doubts.

(STEPHEN *is waiting, refusing to give up.)*

STEPHEN: Have you spoken to Mehta?

ANGELIS: Only on the phone.

STEPHEN: And?

ANGELIS: It is true there are things he does not like in our production.

STEPHEN: Such as?

ANGELIS: I don't know.

STEPHEN: Angelis. Everyone here has heard rumours that the film is in danger.

A MAP OF THE WORLD

(A PROPMAN *has appeared with an inappropriate pink-feathered fan.)*

PROPMAN: Where do I put this?

(There is a sudden quiet. The ELAINE-*actress speaks with authority.)*

ELAINE: Keep going Mike.

(There is a moment before ANGELIS *realizes he must square with the actors. Then:)*

ANGELIS: It is not him. It is Peggy.

STEPHEN: Peggy?

ANGELIS: Peggy came. She visited the set, you remember? Earlier today. She saw the action. It reminds her of the original events—the events, the book, the film. Suddenly she panics. She is now—what?—an older woman, and she sees we are to re-enact a night of which she is no longer proud. Suddenly thinking . . . she realizes she was callous. Her actions seem cruel.

STEPHEN: Right.

ANGELIS: She goes back to Victor Mehta. She tries to stop the film.

STEPHEN: What?

ANGELIS: No, it is fine . . .

*(*ANGELIS *wanders over to the set.)*

ELAINE: The film is being stopped?

ANGELIS: There is a contractual argument, that is all, as to whether Victor Mehta has the right to approve the screenplay.

STEPHEN: Does he?

ANGELIS: In theory, perhaps. It is in his contract, yes, but the lawyers . . . you can imagine.

STEPHEN: Angelis—

ANGELIS: His solicitors have notified us of their intention to serve an injunction, and we have notified them of our intention to counterfile. *(He stops, firm.)* It is a game. *(Then smiles, resuming his usual manner.)* So meanwhile, until the resolution, we schedule rehearsal. Yes? Say nothing please.

A MAP OF THE WORLD

STEPHEN: All right.

(He walks away, unhappily.)

ANGELIS: Please, we rehearse. I beg you, let us act.

(A PROPMAN *has appeared through the 'door' of the 'room' with an enormous bunch of flowers.)*

PROPMAN: You have flowers?

PEGGY: *(Delighted)* For me?

ANGELIS: No, no flowers. The flowers are downstairs.

(The MEHTA-*actor has walked on and has sat down at the desk in the bedroom, taking his jacket off and putting it over the back of the chair.* PEGGY *has for some time been stretched out on the top of the bed in her latest dressing-gown. They are silent, ready to go.)*

ANGELIS: Madeleine in her place. And Shashi, please . . . to work.

(The room is peaceful, ready for action, but the M'BENGUE-*actor is still standing in the middle.)*

ANGELIS: Er, John . . .

*(*M'BENGUE *turns and looks out.)*

M'BENGUE: 'Slavery'.

ANGELIS: What?

M'BENGUE: 'Slavery' is the word.

(There's a pause. Then he turns and walks silently out of the room.)

ANGELIS: OK.

(Only MEHTA *and* PEGGY *remain. The lights change.* PEGGY, *who is staring at the counterpane, now looks up, and* SCENE SIX *begins.)*

PEGGY: How do you write a book?

MEHTA: *(Without looking up)* Mmm?

PEGGY: I mean, when you start out, do you know what you think?

MEHTA: No.

PEGGY: I don't mean the plot. I'm sure the plot's easy . . .

MEHTA: No, the plot's very hard.

211

PEGGY: Well, all right, the plot's hard. But what you think . . . do you know what you think?

MEHTA: No. *(He turns from writing in his notebook and looks at her.)* The act of writing is the act of discovering what you believe. *(He turns back to his work, smiling slightly.)* How do you act?

PEGGY: *(Smiles at once)* Oh, lord . . .

MEHTA: Well?

PEGGY: I mean, I don't. Not really. I'm not an actress. I'm too conscious. I'm too self-aware. I stand aside.

MEHTA: Does that mean you plan to give it up?

(PEGGY *does not answer. She has already picked up a booklet which is beside her on the bed.)*

PEGGY: Don't you love this country?

MEHTA: Why?

PEGGY: An airline timetable, I was looking . . .

MEHTA: Were you thinking of leaving?

PEGGY: No, listen, what I love about India, the only country in the world where they'd print poetry—here, look, at the bottom of the Kuwait-Delhi airline schedule. A poem. 'Some come to India to find themselves, some come to lose themselves . . .' In an airline schedule? Isn't that a pretty frightening admission?

(He is about to speak seriously but she interrupts him.)

MEHTA: Peggy . . .

PEGGY: No, I wasn't leaving. How could I be leaving? I'm here to make a film.

MEHTA: But?

(A pause. Then she looks away.)

PEGGY: But at lunchtime I did something so stupid that the thought of going down those steps . . .

MEHTA: Ah well, yes.

PEGGY: . . . into that lobby, along that corridor, past those delegates, into that deserted conference hall, for this appalling contest . . .

MEHTA: Yes.

212

PEGGY: . . . when all I want is to spend my time with you.
(A pause. MEHTA *sets aside his notebook.)*
MEHTA: American women, they make me laugh. I am at home.
PEGGY: Well, good.
MEHTA: It is like they pick you up in their lovemaking from wherever they last left off. At once, bang! and they're away. No matter with whom it was last time, if it was someone else, no matter, nevertheless, it is go at once. The passion again. Making love to an American woman, it is like climbing aboard an already moving train.
(PEGGY *smiles and gets off the bed to go to the bathroom.)*
PEGGY: We have needs.
MEHTA: I am sure.
PEGGY: *(Calling as she goes out)* We have no guilt. Americans are unashamed of their needs.
MEHTA: *(Smiles)* Yes.
PEGGY: *(Off)* When an Englishman has an emotion, his first instinct is to repress it. When an American has an emotion, his first instinct . . .
MEHTA: Ah well, yes . . .
PEGGY: *(Off)* They express it!
MEHTA: Usually at length.
PEGGY: *(Off)* Why not?
(MEHTA *sits smiling, contented, happy with* PEGGY *and able to show it clearly now she is out of the room.)*
MEHTA: Always examining their own reactions . . .
PEGGY: *(Off)* Yes.
MEHTA: Always analysing, always telling you what they feel—I think, I feel. Hey—let me tell you what I feel . . .
PEGGY: Sure.
MEHTA: The endless drama of it all.
(PEGGY *reappears at the bathroom door. She has taken off her dressing-gown and has changed into another loose cotton suit.)*
PEGGY: And which is better, tell me, Victor, next to the English? Which is healthier, eh?

213

(He looks at her with great affection.)

MEHTA: You make love like a wounded panther. You are like a paintshop on fire.

(She looks at him. Then raises her eyebrows.)

PEGGY: Well, goodness.

MEHTA: Yes.

PEGGY: Writer, eh?

(He smiles. There is a knock at the door. PEGGY goes to answer it.)

MEHTA: It comes in handy.

PEGGY: Is that what you say to all the girls? 'Thank you, that was wounded-panther-like.'

(She opens the door. A WAITER is standing outside.) Yes?

WAITER: Mr Andrews. He is waiting downstairs.

(PEGGY looks at the WAITER a moment, then nods.)

PEGGY: Thank you.

(She closes the door, stands a moment, her face turned away from MEHTA. Then she turns, walks across to the dressing-table and picks up her hairbrush. Then, casually:) What about you?

MEHTA: What?

PEGGY: Are you thinking of leaving?

MEHTA: No, of course not. I shall stay for this contest tonight.

(There is a slight pause, then both of them speak at once.) Peggy . . .

PEGGY: I don't know. I can't say which of the two of you makes more sense to me. I've never had to choose, you see. Like so many people. I've never made a choice.

(She turns and smiles at him.) Sitting at nights with my professors, eating Angel bars, sure, it was great. Philosophy, that was my major . . . eight arguments as to whether God exists.

MEHTA: Does he?

PEGGY: We never decided.

MEHTA: There you are.

PEGGY: But the game was fun. No question. It felt good, it still

214

feels good, that moment of understanding something. When you understand an idea for the first time. But applying it? Well, that's different, the world not offering so many opportunities for that sort of thing. Arts and humanities! Philosophy! What's the point in America, where the only philosophy you'll ever encounter is the philosophy of making money? In my case taking off T-shirts. In fact, not even taking them off— I'm too up-scale for that. I have only to hint there are situations in which I would show my breasts to certain people, certain *rich* people, that they do indeed exist under there, but for now it's enough to suggest their shape, hint at their shape in a T-shirt. Often it will have to be wet. By soaking my T-shirts in water I make my living. It's true. Little to do with the life of ideas.

(She smiles.) Spoiled. Spoiled doesn't say it, though that's what people say about Americans, and spoiled, I suppose, is what I was till lunchtime, till I made this ridiculous offer. A young idiot's suicidal offer with which she is now going to have to learn to live. Yes?

(She turns and looks at MEHTA.*)*

Well, good luck to you. Debate well, Victor, for on your performance depends . . .

MEHTA: *(Smiles)* Don't tell me.

PEGGY: . . . my future. Tonight.

(They stand at opposite sides of the room looking at each other.)

MEHTA: It's your fault.

PEGGY: Oh, yes.

MEHTA: You with your 'Oh, it doesn't matter who wins.' It does matter. What we believe matters more than anything. This you must learn.

(The WAITER *knocks on the door.* PEGGY *does not move, just calls out, looking at* VICTOR *all the time.)*

PEGGY: Yes!

WAITER: Madam, Mr Andrews is asking why you are not downstairs.

215

A MAP OF THE WORLD

PEGGY: Tell him . . . tell him we are coming. Just one minute.
Mr Mehta is preparing his case.
(MEHTA smiles.)
MEHTA: Kiss me.
PEGGY: No kisses. I am no longer yours. I belong now to the
winner of an argument.
(There is another knock at the door.)
PEGGY: Yes!
(ELAINE opens the door.)
Oh, I'm sorry, Elaine, I thought it was the waiter.
ELAINE: Are you coming down?
(A pause.)
MEHTA: Excuse me.
(MEHTA goes out.)
ELAINE: Do I detect a difference of opinion?
PEGGY: No, you detect a very harsh man.
(She goes to the bathroom with a glass of water.)
ELAINE: Well, you don't have to . . .
PEGGY: Don't have to what?
ELAINE: Go through with it. Have a more urgent appointment.
Tell them you're busy. Tell them you're working.
PEGGY: I'm not.
ELAINE: But just lie.
PEGGY: Lie?
ELAINE: Yes, lie. Don't you do that?
(PEGGY thinks a moment.)
PEGGY: Well, no.
(She goes into the bathroom for her hairbrush.)
ELAINE: My God, how do you manage? Lying's the thing which
makes life possible. You should work for the networks for a
while. I can't imagine a life without lying.
PEGGY: Why do you pretend to be so hard-boiled?
ELAINE: I don't pretend. Are you serious? Trying to get my
bosses interested in anything which happens abroad, do you
think I don't have to threaten and blackmail and *lie?* Ask any

216

journalist. Who cares at all. I do it so's to get something on television about how four-fifths of the planet lives.

PEGGY: But doesn't it drive you crazy? How can you bear it?

ELAINE: By 1990 one American in six will at some time in their life have worked for MacDonalds. Put it like that, I'm doing pretty well.

(They look at each other.)

Tell them you're working.

PEGGY: No. It's too late.

(A pause.)

ELAINE: Are you ready?

PEGGY: Yes.

(ELAINE *crosses and kisses her.*)

ELAINE: Let's go down.

(She turns.) All right?

ANGELIS: *(Off)* Yes. But smile at the end.

(ANGELIS *walks thoughtfully on to the set, the lights change and we are into* SCENE SEVEN.)

ANGELIS: All right. Let's go on. Madeleine?

PEGGY: Yes?

(He turns and sees that the PEGGY-*actress has turned away as if to cry.)*

ANGELIS: Are you all right?

PEGGY: Oh, I'm sorry, I . . .

(ANGELIS *holds up a tactful hand at an approaching* CREW MEMBER.)

ANGELIS: Hold it.

PEGGY: No.

(The MEHTA-*actor has returned and now goes over to comfort her.)*

ELAINE: OK, sweetheart?

PEGGY: Yes . . . no . . . I'm sorry, it's silly. I just . . . I was doing the scene. I'd never really thought about it. She didn't know what she was doing, Peggy didn't know, she did it unthinkingly . . . I mean she was innocent.

217

(She looks at them. Then anticlimactically starts to apologize again.) I don't know, I guess I'd never really thought.

ANGELIS: *(Relieved)* OK, right, take the flat out.

CREWMAN: OK, guv.

(The wall goes, the bed goes, the furniture is taken out. A MAKE-UP GIRL waits with Peggy's shoes. At the very back STEPHEN is seen going through his lines with the SCRIPT GIRL.)

STEPHEN: Once more.

SCRIPT GIRL: Same line.

MAKE-UP GIRL: Miss King?

(The PEGGY-actress goes over to put her shoes on. The MEHTA-actor wanders down near her.)

MEHTA: One doesn't think, I know. I'm just as bad. It's ridiculous. One tries so hard when one's acting to make everything real. And yet here we are surrounded by all this apparatus. It's a paradox. You want it to be real. And yet what chance have you. Don't you think?

PEGGY: Mmm.

(MEHTA nods, as if the problem is solved, and walks away. He passes the ELAINE-actress taking up her seat for the next scene, now with a cup of tea.)

ELAINE: Why doesn't she get on with it?

MEHTA: I don't know.

ELAINE: You don't get paid extra for feeling it.

(ANGELIS has gingerly re-approached PEGGY, who is standing, seemingly still upset, by herself at the side.)

ANGELIS: You *are* all right?

PEGGY: You want me to go on?

ANGELIS: If you don't mind.

PEGGY: No, I don't mind.

(She sweeps to her place, suddenly bitter, and sits down. ELAINE smiles across at her.)

ELAINE: OK, darling?

(ANGELIS stands and surveys the whole scene. He nods at STEPHEN.)

218

ANGELIS: Michael. Go on.

(There is a pause. Then STEPHEN, *with the* SCRIPT GIRL *beside him, starts quietly.)*

STEPHEN: 'The thirst for ideals is at the very heart of things. We may say a people need ideals as they need bread. As great as the need for bread is the need for ideals.'

(STEPHEN *walks up to where the other actors are. The* SCRIPT GIRL *goes out, like a trainer leaving her athlete.)*

'The writer serves that need. He should be happy to serve it.'

(He sits down opposite MEHTA *in formal debating position, and at once, as if on cue,* MEHTA *gets up.* SCENE EIGHT *begins.)*

MEHTA: What nonsense! I cannot listen to this man.

PEGGY: Victor, you have agreed.

MEHTA: I know, I know.

PEGGY: It was you who insisted.

MEHTA: I know what I have done . . .

(He stands glowering across the room at STEPHEN.) I have tied myself to a night of stupidity. *(He turns and walks away.)* At lunchtime when you came to propose this confrontation, yes, I said, fine, because I knew I would win. As I shall win. Because my case is unarguably correct. But I had not reckoned—

PEGGY: Victor!

MEHTA: . . . on the sheer indignity. Even to have to *listen* to such peasant-like ideas.

(STEPHEN *just smiles, calm, not rising to the bait.)*

STEPHEN: You speak all the time as if everything were decided. As if you, Victor Mehta, are a finished human being, and beneath you lies the world with all its intolerable imperfections. As if you were objective and had no part in its emotions. Yet some of its worst emotions you exhibit very clearly.

MEHTA: Such as?

STEPHEN: Jealousy.

MEHTA: What do you mean?

STEPHEN: If I mention a novelist, if I mention Graham Greene . . .

MEHTA: A charlatan. Beneath contempt.

STEPHEN: Ah, well, you see. Exactly.

MEHTA: What?

STEPHEN: Your views on other writers.

MEHTA: No! An objective fact! A buffoon! A fool!

STEPHEN: You see! A ribbon of abuse. Pavlovian. At the very mention of the name.

(MEHTA *looks at him mistrustfully, caught out a little.*)

MEHTA: So?

STEPHEN: So, in matters which truly concern you, you are far from objective. On the contrary, when things come too near to you, then you fight from your own corner . . .

MEHTA: Like everyone.

STEPHEN: You fight those things that truly threaten you. In the way Greene threatens you because he is a good writer.

MEHTA: Balls!

STEPHEN: In the way you will fight tomorrow for the right to make fiction. And why? Why do writers insist on their right to distort reality? You demand it in order to make better jokes.

(MEHTA *looks back at him. Then takes him on, beginning quietly.*)

MEHTA: I was born in Bihar, of good family, my father a schoolteacher who died in middle age. My mother died when I was born. A brick-red, hot village on a plain. Baking in the sun. That was my life for fourteen years, seeking tuition where I could, seeking by the formulation of sentences not to escape from the reality into which I was born, but to set it in order. The setting of things in order, that has always been my aim.

(STEPHEN *looks across to* PEGGY, *but she is listening intently.*) It never occurred to me from that village that I should not one day seek civilization. The heroes of the world are its engineers, its doctors, its legislators—yes, there are things in the old Empire I admired, that I was bound to admire, because it is clear to any man born into boastful chaos that order is desirable, and the agents of that order must be practical men. I went to London, to the university there, to the country where once medicine, education, the law had been practised *sans pareil,* and found instead a country now full of sloth and complacency—oh yes, on that we'd agree—a deceitful, inward-looking ruling class blundering by its racialism and stupidity into Suez. This was bitter for a boy from an Indian village. *(He shrugs slightly.)* It seems when people become prosperous, they lose the urge to improve themselves. Anyone who comes new to a society, as I did, an immigrant, has his priorities clear: to succeed in that society, to seek practical achievement, to educate his children to the highest level. Yet somehow once one or two generations have established their success, their grandchildren rush the other way, to disown that success, to disown its responsibilities, to seek by dressing as savages and eating brown rice to discredit the very civilization their grandfathers worked so hard to create. This seems to me the ultimate cruelty . . .

PEGGY: Yes . . .

MEHTA: . . . the ultimate charade: that the young in the West should dare to turn their faces at this time to the Third World and cast doubt on the value of their own material prosperity. Not content with flaunting its wealth, the West now fashionably pretends that the materialism that has produced this wealth is not a good thing. Well, at least give us a chance to find out, say the poor. For God's sake let us practise this contempt ourselves. Instead of sending the Third World doctors and mechanics, we now send them hippies, and Marxist thinkers, and animal conservationists, and ecologists, and wandering fake Zen Buddhist students, who hasten to reassure the illiterate that theirs is a superior life to that of the West. What hypocrisy! The marriage of the decadent with the primitive, the faithless with the barbarian. Reason overthrown, as it is now overthrown all over the world! An unholy alliance, approved, sanctified and financed by this now futile United Nations.

STEPHEN: Futile? Why futile?

MEHTA: Futile because it no longer does any good.
(He gets up again, shouting) Words! Meaningless words! Documents! So many documents that they boast from New York alone there flow annually United Nations documents which, laid end to end at the Equator, would stretch four times round the world! Yes! Half a billion pages! And this . . . this week one of the year's seven thousand major UN meetings. With working papers, proposals, counter-proposals, records, summaries. A bureaucracy drowning in its own words and suffocating in its own documents. The wastepaper basket is the only instrument of sanity in an otherwise insane organization. Last year a Special Committee on the Rationalization and Organization of the General Assembly was set up to examine the problems of excessive documentation. It produced a report. It was two hundred and nineteen pages long. I ask you, what fiction can there be to compare with this absurdity? What writer could dream up this impossible decadence?
(He stands shaking his head.)
No, there is only one thing I know, and one only: that in this universe of idiocy, the only thing we may rely on is the lone voice—the lone voice of the writer—who speaks only when he has something to say.

STEPHEN: Nonsense!

MEHTA: A voice that is pledged to individual integrity.

STEPHEN: My God! What delusion!

ELAINE: It is a bit rich.

MEHTA: Why? *(He turns. Firmly)* Mankind has one enemy only and it is not poverty. It is self-deception. Yes . . . *(He holds a hand up, anticipating* STEPHEN's *objection.)* That finally is my case against you, Stephen. If Miss le Fanu is to adjudicate . . .

ELAINE: I am.

MEHTA: Then please remember that my cast stands or falls here: that often from the best intentions we tell ourselves lies.

A MAP OF THE WORLD

Here—my God!—a conference run by the United Nations is a monument built to commemorate self-deception on the grandest scale. We would like it to work and so we pretend it does but in our hearts—when we are not on our feet, Stephen, not in rooms where words fly up—in our hearts we know the UN is a palace of lies, run by a bureaucracy whose only interest is in the maintenance of its own prosperity. Forty per cent of UNESCO's income is spent in the administration of its own Paris office. A fact. A fact which I have mentioned in my books and for which I am attacked. I am told to point it out is bloody-minded and—what?—'unhelpful'. And yet to me, I am telling you, not to point it out is worse. *(He stands a moment, nodding.)* Tomorrow I must speak because not to speak is not to be a writer, not to be a man.

(Then he looks away to STEPHEN, *opening his hands as if to say, 'That's it.')* That, there, is where I yield. I have had the floor.

STEPHEN: Indeed.

(STEPHEN *looks at* MEHTA *a moment. Then, when he replies, it is with a new and unsuspected warmth.)* We've pretended, you and I, that the debate between us is not to do with personality, only with issues . . .

MEHTA: That's so.

STEPHEN: But in fact, if I've learnt anything in the last twenty-four hours, it is that no argument is pure, it's always a compound. Partly the situation, partly temper, partly whim . . . sometimes just pulled out of the air and often from the worst motives, Peggy, no offence . . .

PEGGY: I understand. *(She smiles.)*

STEPHEN: I've grown up here. In this hotel. I came like a boy, a 27-year-old boy, and I can't help feeling whichever way the contest falls, I'm going to leave a man, partly because I've grown fond of you, Victor.

MEHTA: *(Deadpan)* Really?

STEPHEN: And I think I've felt . . . some growing generosity from you, too, especially this evening. You've stopped calling me Andrews. You call me Stephen, perhaps because even if you don't agree with me, you nevertheless now recognize me. Perhaps even as an element in yourself.

MEHTA: A sentimental line of argument.

STEPHEN: Yes. If I am to win, I must attack the man.

(PEGGY *looks across to* MEHTA, *slightly alarmed. But* MEHTA *does not react.*)

I am arguing that tomorrow you must go out and denounce your own fiction, because it will be your last remaining chance to rejoin the human race.

(A burst of reaction, even MEHTA *surprised.)*

MEHTA: Oh, that's marvellous.

PEGGY: Gee, I must say.

MEHTA: Well.

ELAINE: It's original.

STEPHEN: Everything you say, everything you propose is from a position of superiority and hopelessness. 'What can one do?' you say, grabbing at one depressing piece of information after another, almost—I put it to you—as if you personally were a man now frightened of hope.

MEHTA: Absurd!

STEPHEN: Oh yes, the gleam that comes into your eye when you have some dismal statistic. 'Sixty-five per cent of people who set out to cross roads get run over,' you say with a satisfied beam, as if their presumption had been justly rewarded. Whereas you, of course . . . The position of the habitual non-road crosser has been wholly vindicated! *(He gestures into the air.)* From way up there you claim to see things clearly. 'The truth,' you say, 'the lone voice.' But in fact your so-called truthfulness is nothing but the projection of your own isolation, and of your own despair. Because you do a job which is lonely and hard, because you spend all day locked in a room, so you project your loneliness on to the world.

MEHTA: No.

STEPHEN: Partly from anger at your own way of life, you try to

discredit the work of other people—out there—a lot of whom
have pleasanter jobs than you.
(He pauses. Then, with a smile) Jealousy . . .
MEHTA: No.
STEPHEN: There is jealousy there. The jealousy of a man who
does not take part, who no longer knows how to take part, but
can only write.
(PEGGY *looks across to* MEHTA, *who has turned away.)*
Oh yes. And the more you write, the more isolated you be-
come. The more frozen.
(There is a pause.)
MEHTA: No.
STEPHEN: *(Smiles)* You come here to this conference not to
publicize your work, or to express your position—what would
be the point? Your position is so complete, so closed, there is
little point in expounding it. No, you come to scrape around—
yes, like the rest of us, to scrape around for contact.
(A pause. Then PEGGY *suddenly seems embarrassed, con-
fused.)*
PEGGY: No, please, it's . . .
STEPHEN: What?
PEGGY: Unfair.
STEPHEN: Why?
(STEPHEN *turns back,* MEHTA *himself still impassive.)*
STEPHEN: Why?
(STEPHEN *turns back,* MEHTA *himself still impassive.)* Your
wife, your child, you leave behind in England . . .
(He looks quickly to PEGGY, *who plainly knows nothing of
wife or child.)*
Oh yes. Come here. Five thousand miles. Make love to Peggy
Whitton. Leave. The last emotions left. Jealousy, yes. And
lust. What is left in you that is not disdainful, that is not dead?
Only jealousy and lust.
(There is a silence. ELAINE *looks between them, warning.)*
ELAINE: Look, Stephen . . .
(But STEPHEN *is leaning forward to make his main point.)*

STEPHEN: You will never understand any struggle unless you take part in it. How easy to condemn this organization as absurd. Of course I've sat here and sweated and bitched and argued . . . often with Elaine . . .

ELAINE: It's true.

STEPHEN: I've run screaming from the points of order and the endless 'I am mandated to ask . . .' But why do you not think that at the centre of the verbiage, often only by hazard but nevertheless at times and unpredictably, crises are averted, aid is directed?

MEHTA: I dare say.

STEPHEN: Why do you not imagine that if you stopped distancing yourself, if you got rid of your wretched fastidiousness, you could not lend yourself for once not to objection but to getting something done?

(STEPHEN *sits back, contemptuous.*)

Oh, no, it's too hard. Never—the risk of failure too great. Like so many clever men, you move steadily to the right, further, further, distancing, always distancing yourself, building yourself a bunker into which only the odd woman is occasionally allowed, disowning your former ideals . . .

MEHTA: You know nothing.

STEPHEN: . . . attacking those who still have those ideals with a ferocity which is way out of proportion to their crime.

(MEHTA *is suddenly stirred.*)

MEHTA: No!

STEPHEN: Yes! Well, move, move to the right if you wish to. Join the shabby crew if you want to. Go in the way people do. But at least spare us the books, spare us the Stations of the Cross, the public announcements. Make your move in private, do it in private, like a sexual pervert, do it privately. Move with a mac over your knee to the right, but spare us, spare your audience, spare those who have to watch one good man after another go down.

PEGGY: Stephen, it is too much.

ELAINE: Please.

STEPHEN: No!

(He has stood up.) The revenge of the old! All the time! The history of the world is the revenge of the old, as they paint themselves into corners, loveless, removed, relieved occasionally in hotel rooms by the visits of strange women, who come to tell them that, yes, they are doing well and, yes, they may now take revenge on those who are still young. People, countries, the same thing; the world now full of young countries who are trying imperfect, unwieldy new systems of ordering their affairs, watched by the old who are praying that they will not succeed . . . *(He shakes his head. Then suddenly)* If you wish to rejoin us, if you wish to be human, go out tomorrow and parrot whatever rubbish you are handed and at least experience an emotion which is not disdain.

MEHTA: I would not give you the pleasure.

STEPHEN: I shall not be here.

MEHTA: What?

STEPHEN: A midnight train leaves for Ahmadabad and on to Jaipur. Frankly . . . *(He smiles and crosses the room.)* . . . my time is being wasted here.

ELAINE: Stephen . . .

(STEPHEN has collected his abandoned briefcase.)

PEGGY: What are you doing?

(STEPHEN has turned to PEGGY.)

STEPHEN: Peggy, I'm sorry. Your offer, it was kind, more than tempting. But all afternoon, all evening, I realized . . . also absurd. My own fault. For years I've apologized. A shambler, a neurotic, I've accepted the picture the world has of an idealist as a man who is necessarily a clown. No shortage of people to tell him he's a fool. And we accept this picture. Yes, we betray our instincts. We betray them because we're embarrassed, and we've lost our conviction that we can make what's best in us prevail.

(He smiles, his briefcase closed, and he is now ready to go.) Well, enough—I'm sorry—

PEGGY: *(Smiles)* Stephen . . .

227

STEPHEN: . . . of all that.

(He takes her hand a moment.)

No more apology. Hold to my beliefs.

(He turns to ELAINE.) Elaine, I owe you lunch.

ELAINE: *(Getting up to embrace him)* Stephen . . .

STEPHEN: Thank you. Send my best to America. I withdraw from the contest. What you must do only you can decide. *(He turns and goes out. The three of them left behind. There is silence.* MEHTA *looks down at the envelope in his hand. Toys with it a moment.)*

MEHTA: *(Darkly)* I should not have come here. I am going upstairs.

(He goes out. The two women are left alone on the stage. PEGGY *looks down.)*

PEGGY: Now I'm going to get drunk.

(And as she looks up, the lights fade to darkness, as much like a film fade as possible. There is a pause in the dark. Then the sound of banging at the back. From far away MEHTA's *voice, a stick beating at the door, and* SCENE NINE *has begun.)*

MEHTA: Hello. Please. Is there anyone?

(At once, in the darkness, the sound of an ASSISTANT *scurrying across the set.)*

ASSISTANT: Coming! Coming!

(At the very back of the stage, far further than we realized the stage reached, a door opens, and brilliant light pours through it. Silhouetted in the doorway stands MEHTA.)

MEHTA: I am Victor Mehta.

ASSISTANT: Ah, yes. You were expected earlier.

(He turns, panicking slightly.)

Everyone! Please! Is there a light there!

(He turns to MEHTA.) Please wait.

MEHTA: I am waiting.

(A single light comes on in the grid and we see the stage is now black. An empty film studio. ANGELIS *is rushing on, in the last stages of pulling his trousers up.)*

228

ANGELIS: Ah, my goodness, you are here. We were expecting you earlier.

(MEHTA *has come right down. He is a more formidable man in a camelhair coat, heavier, less dapper.* ANGELIS *shakes his hand.*) An honour.

MEHTA: You are pulling on your trousers.

ANGELIS: A friend.

(He elaborates needlessly, embarrassed) In make-up.

MEHTA: I see.

ANGELIS: A drink?

(An ASSISTANT *has brought a chair, but* MEHTA *has wandered away.)*

MEHTA: Mr. Angelis, I cannot pretend I am glad to come here.

ANGELIS: You have read the script?

MEHTA: I cannot read five pages.

ANGELIS: *(To his* ASSISTANT) Thank you.

(The ASSISTANT *goes.)*

No, well, admittedly . . . there are weaknesses—

MEHTA: The dialogue. When they open their mouths, dead frogs fall out.

ANGELIS: Yes, well, certainly . . . it can do with polishing . . .

MEHTA: A moral story has been reduced to the status of a romance, transferred to a vulgar medium and traduced. Very well. It is what one expects. One looks to the cinema for money, not for enlightenment. And to be fair, the money has arrived.

(He turns and faces ANGELIS.)

It is in the matter of meaning I have come.

ANGELIS: Meaning?

MEHTA: Meaning, Mr Angelis.

ANGELIS: Ah, yes.

(MEHTA looks at him. Then starts afresh.)

MEHTA: There is a balance in the book. Each of the characters is forced to examine the values of his or her life.

ANGELIS: Yes.

MEHTA: The novelist is accused of dalliance and asked to put a value on what he has seen as a passing affair. The actress questions her easy promiscuity and is made to realize adulthood will involve choice. And Stephen, the journalist, assumes the confidence of his own beliefs.

ANGELIS: And is killed.

MEHTA: Killed, yes.

(There is a pause.)

You show this?

ANGELIS: Of course. We have a train.

(MEHTA *looks at him. Another pause.)*

MEHTA: In a sense, I care nothing. A book is written. It is left behind you to be misinterpreted by a thousand critics. The reader brings to the book his own preconceptions, prejudices perhaps. He misreads sentences. A tiny incident in the narrative is for one person the key to the book's interpretation; to another it is where he accidentally turns two pages and misses it altogether. So if you come, if you make a film, you'll reinterpret. And yet, in spite of that, your film is a betrayal unless at the heart it is clear: for all the bitterness, for all the stupidity . . . you must see, we admired this young man.

(A pause. MEHTA *sits back.)*

Of course, death, death brings him dignity, but also in truth, even at the time . . .

(MEHTA *looks away.* ANGELIS *waits tactfully.)*

ANGELIS: Yes, well, that's clear.

MEHTA: Clear to you, perhaps. Yes, your intention. But is it there in the script? Peggy didn't see it when she visited this morning.

ANGELIS: I see. Is that all?

MEHTA: No. The death.

ANGELIS: Ah.

MEHTA: And the way you tell it.

ANGELIS: I see.

MEHTA: There is something there. An emotion I had.

(There is a pause. Then, soberly) Certainly we drove, as you suggest it. Peggy heard first. She was awoken at six and came

to my room. We found a taxi-driver. All the way from Bombay he smoked marijuana. Thirty miles out Peggy and I demanded to change cabs. Another drive, the day beginning to get hot. And we knew, long before we reached the disaster, just how close the disaster was. Small groups of people at first; driving further, more people. Now in larger groups, now more excited, finally crowds, in the middle of the valley. A valley like any other but for the crowds. We had expected a corpse. A body on its own, we had thought. It was impossible even to get close to the carriages which had overturned. All one side, people had clung to the framework and been crushed. A single cow had strayed on to the line. Forty more miles to the mortuary . . . to unidentified bodies . . . paperwork . . . hysteria . . . the heat. And the conference itself was suddenly rendered ridiculous. Whatever meaning it once had was now lost. As tomorrow . . . in this barn, the lights will burn, the camera will turn, a predetermined script will be acted out by men and women who know it has been robbed of sense.

(He nods.)

The machine turns of its own volition! Oh, the will that is needed to bring it to a halt!

(He smiles, bitter.) I was not there, and M'Bengue denounced me. Yes! In savage terms. 'This fascist novelist, this charlatan, who, when the moment comes, ducks the chance to defend his indefensible work . . .'

(A pause.)

I was not there. I was at the accident.

ANGELIS: Of course.

(A silence. ANGELIS *uneasy.)*

But surely when people realized, I mean, your reason, why you weren't there . . .

MEHTA: Why should they care? The whole conference was longing for a dogfight. What a disappointment when it did not occur.

No, the book is clear. I was moved by what happened, and

later that day I made a choice. The conference could continue without me. This you do not mention but you must make it clear. I chose to be silent. In memory of Stephen . . . I stayed away.

ANGELIS: I see. Yes. I'd not understood that. If what you're after is this feeling that everything is meaningless, then, of course, we will put that in as well. A slight dialogue adjustment, a page maybe. Then it is clear.

(There is a pause. The STEPHEN-*actor has appeared at the back, dressed in baggy trousers and an expensive coat. Soft-spoken. The* PEGGY-*actress is standing behind him, dressed very young in a smart coat and jeans.)*

STEPHEN: Oh, I'm sorry. Are we interrupting?

ANGELIS: Michael . . .

STEPHEN: We were half-way to Belgravia before I realized I'd forgotten . . .

*(*MEHTA *is staring at him.)*

MEHTA: You are he.

STEPHEN: . . . my script.

(Then STEPHEN *makes a formal move towards* MEHTA, *the* PEGGY-*actress following a little nervously behind.)*

Mr Mehta?

(He turns to introduce the PEGGY-*actress but* MEHTA, *over-come, has turned away, not taking his hand.)*

Madeleine . . .

MEHTA: I am sorry.

(The other three stand, uncertain. PEGGY *and* STEPHEN *look fresh and scrubbed and absurdly young.* STEPHEN *looks nervously to* ANGELIS.)*

STEPHEN: Angelis, here, said you weren't happy with the text.

MEHTA: I cannot begin to say. Everything is wrong.

(He turns back, recovering. STEPHEN *at his most diffident and charming.)*

STEPHEN: I can see from the outside it must be discomforting. Film is.

(MEHTA *looks at him with respect.* PEGGY, *emboldened, smiles.)*

PEGGY: We can't be doing what you want, Mr Mehta. We're aware of it, ours is bound to be a love story. A commercial picture with, eventually, after the studio, some exotic locations. Sex and death are really the standout features, rather than the arguments in the book, some of which we are filming . . . all of which, I guess, we think, will be cut.

(They smile, only ANGELIS *uneasy.)*

ANGELIS: This is, by any prevailing standard, is a picture of integrity.

PEGGY: Can you imagine?

STEPHEN: Even though they've put in a scene where Elaine bathes topless in the holy river.

PEGGY: It's true. It's hard to believe.

STEPHEN: Two thousand Indians in dhotis and she takes her top off. A reporter? From CBS?

(ANGELIS *looks silently resentful.)*

PEGGY: Quite apart from how the holy river . . .

MEHTA: It is not in Bombay.

STEPHEN: Quite. It's a thousand miles away. That small detail apart . . .

(ANGELIS *sulky on his own, as the others smile.)*

ANGELIS: It is not true. She is to bathe in the tank.

(STEPHEN *points to his own forehead.)*

STEPHEN: We have this book here, however.

MEHTA: Thank you.

STEPHEN: In our heads. This blunderer . . . *(He gestures amiably at* ANGELIS.) Me, an actor of limited ability. Madeleine, God bless her, who is reading Herodotus—can you imagine? —to get into the part.

(The PEGGY-*actress blushes and looks at her feet.)*

'Reading Herodotus?' I said casually one day. 'Oh, you know,' she said, 'just skimming.'

(MEHTA *smiles, touched.)*

All the warmth, all the kindness we can bring, we will bring.

MEHTA: Thank you. That is something. I suppose.

(He stands a moment, the whole group still. Then, resigned:)
For the rest, of course, let it be toplessness.

STEPHEN: What else?

MEHTA: And bad dialogue. What else?

PEGGY: No sauna scene so far, but we're expecting one.

(MEHTA nods slightly, the joke shared. Then STEPHEN makes to go.)

STEPHEN: If you like, I can drive you back to London.

MEHTA: That will be good.

STEPHEN: I'll just get my things.

(He goes out to the dressing-rooms.)

PEGGY: Excuse me.

(PEGGY follows him.)

MEHTA: Mr Angelis, farewell. Thank you for listening.

ANGELIS: No.

(He shakes MEHTA's hand.)
If we can do it as you wish, we shall be pleased.

(He goes out. MEHTA is left momentarily alone on the huge, empty stage. Then he turns his head and at once MARTINSON walks on, eerily quiet, and, from the other direction, M'BENGUE. SCENE TEN. The lights change. A sinister calm.)

MARTINSON: Monsieur M'Bengue . . .

(The two men stand still opposite each other, formally, in the centre of the stage.)
Your speech was excellent.

M'BENGUE: Yes. I admired this young man. So few whites have any understanding.

MARTINSON: The occasion was perfectly handled. And in a way, although tragic—the tragedy eats into my soul—but also, we must say, the way things fell out has also been elegant.

M'BENGUE: Elegant?

MARTINSON: Convenient.

(M'BENGUE looks at him with silent contempt.)

M'BENGUE: I see.

MARTINSON: Mr Mehta's necessary absence certainly removed the problems we had had.

(M'BENGUE *looks at him a moment, still quiet, still calm.*)

M'BENGUE: Mr Martinson, overnight I have been reading the conditions, the terms, of the aid you are proposing to give. They are stiff.

MARTINSON: They are exacting, yes. No aid is pure. There is always an element of trade in all such arrangements, and trade, after all, benefits both sides.

M'BENGUE: Surplus corn, surplus grain from America, at a commercial price . . .

MARTINSON: Less than the market price.

M'BENGUE: A considerable price.

(MARTINSON *smiles.*)

MARTINSON: Perhaps.

M'BENGUE: The other part of the package, the facility of a loan from the World Bank.

MARTINSON: That's right.

M'BENGUE: At 13 per cent. And not even that is the limit of it. With it a demand for changes in the internal policies of our country . . .

MARTINSON: Adjustments, yes.

M'BENGUE: . . . deflation of the currency . . .

MARTINSON: Well . . .

M'BENGUE: . . . high internal interest rates.

MARTINSON: Strict monetary measures. *(He smiles again.)* Good housekeeping, yes.

M'BENGUE: A recognition that younger countries cannot expect to have social security systems. In sum, the destruction of the policies which brought our government into being. You throw us a lifeline. The lifeline is in the shape of a noose.

(MARTINSON *shrugs slightly.*)

MARTINSON: Well, I think you will find it's not necessarily that sinister. Certainly, over the five-year period the bank is insisting, for its own protection, on certain parameters—is that the word? There may well be some hardship at first. A largely agricultural country like your own, peasant-based one would expect things to be hard when such measures are introduced. Five years', ten years' belt-tightening. Suffering. Comparative. Then, well, surely . . . you'll be out of the woods. *(He gestures to one side.)* Shall we go through? There's a final dinner. We were going to have pheasant, but it was generally felt, for a symbolic gesture, it being the last night, each one of us will eat a single bowl of rice. I hope it's all right. *(He is about to go.)* Oh, by the way, you will not refuse it?

M'BENGUE: The loan I cannot. I shan't eat the rice.

(M'BENGUE *turns and goes out.* MARTINSON, *left alone, turns and goes out the other way.* MEHTA *stands alone, then the* PEGGY-*actress reappears at the other side of the stage. He smiles absently at her. There is an embarrassed silence between them,* MEHTA *still thinking about the scene which has just passed.)*

MEHTA: Do you have children?

PEGGY: Oh, no. No, I don't. You have a son?

MEHTA: By my first marriage, yes. I have custody. He lives with Peggy and me. He's sixteen. A boy. He wants to change the world.

PEGGY: Well, I guess . . . that's the best thing to do with it. *(The actress smiles.)* I'd like to meet him.

MEHTA: And he no doubt you.

(He stands a moment.)

This feeling, finally, that we may change things—this is at the centre of everything we are. Lose that . . . lose that, lose everything.

(He stands, the man who has.)

PEGGY: I'm sorry. I didn't catch what you said.

(The STEPHEN-*actor returns, yet more cheerful than before.)*

STEPHEN: I have an open car. I hope that's all right. It can be a bit cold. It's a steel-grey, 2.4 litre 1954 Alvis. A Grey Lady. With real running-boards. Like this. Not very practical for the English winter. But it is so beautiful.

(He looks at MEHTA.) It's my whole life.

236

MEHTA: Yes. I am sure.
(Distantly, music begins to play. MEHTA *moves a few paces towards the door, then turns, suddenly cheered.)* Madeleine. Michael. To London. Let's go.
(He lifts his arms, the music swells and the lights go out.)